Taming Your Tiger Mom

TAKE BACK YOUR FUTURE AND LIVE THE LIFE YOU WANT

Tim Pitts

ISBN-13: 9780692591604
ISBN-10: 0692591605
Library of Congress Control Number: 2015920073
Jack Dog Publishing, Savannah, GA

Dedicated to my wife
Ellen Holl Pitts.
Who knew?

Table of Contents

Life is all about a time and a place, we aren't here to figure it out...just to be open to it.
Kristey King

CHAPTER 1
No Regrets

Anyone who says he has no regrets is either living in denial or utterly blind to his missed possibilities and opportunities. I have plenty of regrets, among which are that I missed Woodstock and made the second call to my first wife.

One of my biggest regrets is that I never made a career out of any of my interests. Instead, after graduating from college I chose a respectable career as an insurance agent and spent three and a half years hating what I did.

To be perfectly transparent, I should say that few of my high school teachers would have predicted that I'd be successful at anything. On graduation day the headmaster told my father that while life for me would be difficult, he hoped I'd make the best of what I had. If his comment wasn't particularly encouraging, I hadn't given him reason to expect much more. I was interested in lots of things, just not the things in which teachers wanted me to be interested.

College was a disaster. My collegiate career began in 1968, the same year that hell was breaking out on campuses all over America. Sex, drugs, and vending machines filled with beer. I was a hyperactive kid in an ADD candy store. Four years and two summer schools later, I graduated near the bottom of my class with a degree in history, arguably no better schooled than when I arrived.

Not surprisingly I never thought much about what I'd do after graduation. In an era marked by confusion, protest, violence, and, for some students, a profound sense of apathy, planning for the future wasn't a priority. "Carpe diem" and "never trust anyone over thirty" were popular youth dictates. We swore we'd never be "the man," whatever that meant.

We lived the mantra that "less is best." I graduated and returned home with all of my possessions stuffed into two Kroger shopping bags. But once we graduated few of us carried minimalism and protest into adulthood. We stuffed bell-bottoms, boots, and bongs into the backs of closets and replaced them with off-the-rack suits, club ties, and occasionally shined shoes. Most of us interviewed for jobs without giving much thought to what we really wanted to do.

My father was not subtle in expressing his wish that I join the family business. Not wanting to disappoint him, and without alternatives, I acquiesced. It took less than a day to realize I'd made a terrible mistake. What I signed on for in no way reflected my interests. In short, I entered the insurance business without taking the time to consider who I was, what I liked, and how I ultimately wanted to spend my life.

After a few years of misery I abandoned insurance and jumped to investments. For the next twenty-three years, I plied my trade as a stockbroker, branch manager, sales manager, and finally, chairman of the sales subsidiary of OppenheimerFunds. While I enjoyed a successful career I often sensed something was missing.

In 1998 I left the investment business, and for two years lived a dream. I combined my passions for photography, history, current events, and travel to become a freelance photojournalist. Two years, several articles, and a couple of photography shows later, I became a history teacher at The Hun School of Princeton.

—— ∞∞ ——

It was as a teacher that I first became aware of a serious problem affecting you and the future of our country. As a teacher I learned the extent to which your parents are failing to prepare you for the leadership roles you will be asked to assume in the future.

Your parents' manic quest to fill every moment with activities designed to make you more attractive to colleges is depriving you of important opportunities for self-discovery.

The Great Recession of 2008 exposed the failure. Before the nation's financial crisis, it was relatively easy for college graduates to find work. As entry-level jobs became difficult to find, parents who knew of my previous career occasionally asked if I'd help their recent graduates find jobs. In response, I created Shameless Self Promotion, a small career coaching business for college students and recent graduates. Before long I detected a disturbing pattern. Those I coached had little vision of what they wanted in their careers and almost no idea how to pursue them if they did.

I concluded that a systemic and troubling trend is infecting students. Many seem risk averse, uncertain of their problem-solving skills, overly provincial, and clueless about how interests or passions might factor into the equation. Surprisingly few individuals with whom I met were focused or able to communicate their goals effectively.

The problem begins with parents who believe that competition for college and jobs after graduation trump personal discovery. They believe it is necessary for you to take courses that enhance your transcripts rather than feed your interests or foster self-exploration. They appeal to teachers for better grades on report cards and complain if coaches don't give you enough playing time. It doesn't matter that you didn't deserve a better grade or didn't have the skills to warrant more time on the field. This is not a recipe for training future leaders.

Many parents insist that you take the "right classes" so that you can get into the "right colleges" in order to get the "right jobs." You don't always get a vote in the matter. You are steered in one direction or another without regard to your interests or desires. Sports, travel sports, after-school activities, and gargantuan amounts of homework, rob you of time to come to grips with you. It is no wonder you have so little opportunity to discover yourselves.

It's helicoptering on steroids, and parents aren't the only ones who are guilty: schools, college counselors, and college administration and faculty are part of the problem. It's no wonder so many of you are unsure of what you want to do after graduation.

Many of you talked to me about the frustrations you felt when you wanted to take courses that sounded interesting, only to have your parents insist that you take something else because it might have more cachet to a college admissions office. I once asked an extremely artistic student what she wanted to major in. She told me that while she "really, really" wanted to major in art history, her mother, an economist, insisted that she major in economics because it would open doors to myriad job opportunities. Nothing about majoring in economics appealed to the student who "really, really" wanted to study art history.

Yet another student, a junior in high school, told me his father was already pressuring him to major in business administration to prepare him to enter the family business after graduation.

During one memorable parent-teacher conference, a parent actually told me that his daughter's future was limited if she didn't get into an Ivy League school. One can only imagine the sense of failure the student would have felt if she did not go Ivy.

The solution to the problem requires that you and your parents forge a different relationship. You want your parents to flatten the hierarchal family structure, lengthen your leash, and encourage you to accept risk. It's mentorship 101.

Being your puppet master does not prepare you to be a thoughtful leader. Being your mentor will.

Eliminating risk and solving problems for you deprives you of the opportunity to develop important life skills. On some level you already know that actions involve risks, and failure is part of the learning process. Embrace that knowledge. Doubt conventional thinking, effectively argue your conclusions, and clearly communicate your point of view. Use ingenuity to solve your own problems.

In one sense education is a means to an end. The endgame is achieved when *you* land a meaningful job in the career of *your* own choosing; the career that best reflects *your* interests and accommodates *your* unique skills. As mentors and allies, you parents can help you succeed by identifying careers that are right for you.

Achieving an important endgame is accomplishing a major goal. It is a big endeavor, requiring focus, careful preparation, and training. Recent statistics suggest that even as the worst recession since the Great Depression is behind us, your employment outlook remains cloudy. The economy continues to improve, but the unemployment rate for Americans under age twenty-five remains more than double the overall unemployment rate.

To avoid the frustration of unemployment and the indignity of moving back in with your parents, you need to prepare yourself to meet the challenges of finding a job after graduation. Despite skyrocketing tuitions, few colleges invest what is needed to develop effective career counseling for students. Given today's tuitions it is reasonable to expect colleges and universities to do more to help. Until they do your parents have to assume the primary responsibility for preparing you for life after college. They can't abdicate this burden to anyone else. In the final analysis, the environment in which a student is raised does more than anything else to pave the road to success.

A culture for success is one in which your parents mentor, and you learn and practice the life skills you need in order to be successful. By leading more than managing, carefully observing you as you discover your individual skills and interests, anticipating mistakes, promoting trial and error, and encouraging you to pursue your passions, your parents empower you to succeed. Anything less works against you in the long run.

Many parents confuse micromanagement—think helicopter parenting, bulldozing, and tiger moms—with leadership. Overscheduling, overindulging, over-orchestrating, and over-parenting are not examples of effective leadership. On the contrary, if this practice is supposed to help you hold your own in an increasingly competitive world, it is having the opposite effect.

More often than not, those who get coveted jobs after graduation are raised in family cultures that value and foster creativity and discovery. These cultures encourage risk, are goal oriented and collaborative.

If you are raised in a culture like this you learn to disagree, debate, and negotiate all in the spirit of achieving results that best serve everyone involved.

Getting back on track will require change. Change is never easy. It is important that you to start now. A culture that encourages you to discover your passions and skills will pave the way for success in the future and ensure the American dream will remain intact for future generations.

Stay motivated. Remember -- No Regrets!

The Bottom Line

- Everyone has regrets. Your career choice doesn't have to be one of them.
- The recession of 2008 changed the job market landscape for recent college graduates.
- You are not being adequately prepared for the leadership roles you will be asked to assume in the future.
- Too many students are unable to communicate their goals effectively, often because they lack a well-defined vision of their own future.
- Unfortunately competition to get into the "right college," in order to get the "right job," now trumps personal discovery.
- Eliminating risk and solving problems for you deprives you of the opportunity to develop important life skills.
- Don't be frustrated; there are solutions.
- A culture for success is one in which your parents mentor, and you learn and practice the life skills you need in order to succeed.
- Avoid regrets by staying focused on what's right for you.
- Always remember: your future belongs to you.
- Take charge.

CHAPTER 2
It's A Different World

M att was frustrated. A recent graduate, he'd been trying unsuccessfully to find a job: no bites, no nibbles, nothing. He wasn't prepared for the new realities of finding meaning employment after graduation. He'd never been schooled in the basic skills he needed to compete successfully: skills like personal branding, networking, and interviewing. These skills didn't seem so important when the job market was strong, but as the economy cooled and jobs became scarcer they became critical.

A political science major with a minor in business, Matt sent his résumé "all over the place." He rarely got a response. He had a few screening interviews but none resulted in a second round. "I feel like such a loser. I have no idea what to do."

Matt is not a loser and it wasn't his fault that he was having so much trouble. A few years earlier, when there was a job surplus, he would have found a job fairly quickly. That was then. By the time he graduated things were different.

There is an old saying on Wall Street that bull markets mask bad management. It is an unfortunate reality that when a company is doing well -- sales are strong, and its stock is in record territory -- it is very easy for management to take its eyes off of the fundamentals. Costs creep upward, variable expenses increase, and hiring grows as if the good times will last forever. It's as if collective amnesia infects decision makers, who convince themselves this bull market is different: the good times will keep on rolling.

When times are good, skills are too frequently subordinated to expediency in the rush to fill open positions. When the economy is weak, hiring managers become far more selective in the interview process. Applicants who are prepared have a leg up.

Matt learned that he didn't have to do anything out of the ordinary in order to land a job. By applying certain basic principles, he eventually found a position in a career that utilized his skill sets and interests. In order to bridge the gap between feeling like a loser and the sweet smell of success, he had to be clear on what he really wanted to do. Then he had to be clear about himself -- his vision, persona, skills, interests, and ambitions.

Matt needed a mission and goals. When he applied for a job he needed to understand the role for which he was applying, and how he could add value. He even had to adopt the dress code, language, and mannerisms of someone who did that job so that a hiring manager could visualize him in the role. Before that however, Matt needed to learn networking and interview skills.

When I first met Matt, he didn't have a clear idea of what he wanted to do. As a result his résumé wasn't structured to reflect any career-specific experience, and his cover letter lacked focus. Further, he had never learned the nuances of effective networking or winning interview techniques. Like many recent graduates, Matt did not understand that he was a salesperson with a single product: himself. Whether or not he ultimately wanted a career in sales was immaterial; he had to utilize proven sales techniques to be a successful interviewer.

For Matt to create value, he first had to know and be comfortable with himself. He had to know his strengths, appreciate his weaknesses, and know how best to communicate his skills. He also needed to focus on what he really wanted to do. The shotgun approach, or chasing any position for the sake of getting a job, creates too many distractions and often results in a job you don't really want. This meant Matt needed to create a list of prospective organizations and individuals in the field in which he wanted to start his career. This required extensive research in order to gain important background knowledge and basic intelligence.

Once Matt focused on the career he wanted he began creating meaningful goals and developed steps to achieve them. The more he researched, the more confident he became. As his confidence grew, he gained some control over his destiny and quickly found a meaningful position in the career that best utilized his interests and assets.

Before the global economy turned on its head in 2008, very few people were prescient enough to suggest that a correction was inevitable, that the good times might end. Subsequently, when it did collapse, few were prepared to deal with the new realities. Students were confident of their abilities to find jobs, and their parents had no reason to question that confidence. The global economy was booming, in part driven by new technologies that connected us in ways that guaranteed exciting opportunities for graduates. There was no reason to believe that things wouldn't be different this time.

Things were different; new, potentially corrosive realities crept into our lives almost unnoticed as we labored under the illusion that American economic hegemony was sacrosanct.

Emerging economies, the global education explosion, the technology revolution, and universally accessible information are exciting game changers. However, in our zeal to embrace a rapidly changing world, too many of us have failed to remember that change is a two-edged sword.

We forget that new technologies replace old; those of us stubbornly adhering to the past risk becoming obsolete. America's transforming job market has led students and their parents to discover another new reality: the way we prepare students to land jobs and launch their careers no longer works. The present has little in common with the past.

Many parents, using their own experience as a guide, believe college graduation is the endgame; the point where their responsibility ends and their family payroll shrinks. That's no longer true. College is no longer the endgame; a degree does not in and of itself provide the skills one needs in order to get a job. Today the goal has shifted to meaningful employment after college. This requires students to acquire skills above and beyond course content.

Generally speaking, in the post–World War II era in America, being a college graduate meant being employed. Most often graduates found a job surplus when they exited the hallowed halls and, with rare exception, were able to find positions in the careers they wanted. That was the reality until the world began to change. China's shift to a market economy in the late 1970s and the demise of the Soviet Union in 1991 should have raised red flags—but they didn't.

The recent emphasis placed on education in developing countries has created a large, well-trained global labor pool. Add to this the technology explosion and universal access to information, and today's graduates face a difficult environment. Jobs that used to go almost exclusively to Americans are now open to capable, well-educated, motivated students from all corners of the globe. Employers can't be faulted for seeking the best talent available regardless of political borders.

These new realities mean competition for jobs is far more intense than ever before. Graduates need to meet the challenge. But to do so they need help and too many are not getting the help they need.

Parents are uniquely positioned to help their children, yet many seem unsure of how to do so. There is a critical disconnect between how college prepares students to find jobs in careers for which they have prepared and their ability to do so. Most colleges don't adequately provide students with the skills they need to put all they learn in school to practical use, including salesmanship, networking, and interviewing. Career centers, which are understaffed by individuals with little or no experience in hiring or in meeting a payroll, help students with résumés and cover letters before pointing them in the direction of Monster.com.

In today's world trying to find a job by sending your résumé is taking a shotgun approach when

careful aim is needed. In short it's a fool's game.

The problem is not job availability. While the face of the job market has changed, there are still excellent jobs waiting to be filled. The challenges involved in finding a job today require changing tactics, and new tactics require new skills.

If frustration is understandable, it is also avoidable. Blindly submitting résumés used to be the way we applied for jobs. Today that is an almost guaranteed route to frustration and disappointment.

There are exceptions. Jack, a business major, sent his résumé to Bloomberg in response to a job advertisement in his junior year, when he was in Barcelona for a semester-abroad program. He received a response and conducted his interview via Skype, and the company offered him a summer internship.

According to Jack, "I was amazed. Most of my friends really struggled to find anything, but for me it clicked. The great thing is that at the end of the summer, Bloomberg offered me a job starting the following June, so I began my senior year knowing I had a job doing what I wanted to do when I graduated."

Jack is the exception. Today there are so many students submitting résumés for available positions, it's become a game of chance. The process of vetting résumés has been so dehumanized that unless one believes that a computer can reliably decide one's future, relying on this tactic alone to find a job is an exercise in futility. The surest way to the career you want is getting in front of people who can help. That means learning how to network effectively.

In the second half of the twentieth century, the United States seemed almost impervious to competition. To be sure there were a few troubling hiccups along the way. But for most of that time, Americans had plenty of reasons to feel smug about our position in the global arena.

For the vast majority of Americans coming of age in the second half of the century, it was like hitting a lottery. America and Americans were different; the world coveted our standard of living. But in the last ten years, as differences have narrowed, the infallibility of the American dream no longer seems secure. In fact the dream is no longer uniquely American; it is global. The American dream is no longer a given.

Today America is competing with countries and regions that didn't even register on the economic Richter scale a scant twenty years ago. Today we are competing for jobs that didn't exist five years ago, and college freshmen are preparing for jobs that haven't been invented, using technology that will be obsolete by the time they graduate.

When your parents graduated from college, finding a meaningful career was not particularly difficult. Plenty of jobs were available, and there was a high likelihood that they'd find an entry-level position in their chosen career.

That was then.

The Bottom Line

- The American Dream is no longer a given.
- In a weak economy, hiring managers become far more selective in the interview process.
- The same is true when the available pool of skilled applicants is large, growing, and global.
- Today you compete with an available, global, well educated and well trained labor force.
- Employers can't be faulted for seeking the best talent available, regardless of political boundaries.
- The challenges involved in finding a job today require changing tactics, and new tactics require new skills.
- Develop and define your mission.
- When you consider career options, focus on what your really want to do.
- Once focused, create meaningful goals and develop steps to achieve them.
- Know yourself... your vision, persona, skills, interests, and ambitions.
- Know, and be able to demonstrate, how you add value.

CHATPER 3
How It's Different

Lisa was frustrated. Her daughter, Teresa, an honors student, graduated seven months earlier and, despite all her efforts, had not yet found a job.

"I don't get it," said Lisa. "We spent almost two hundred thousand dollars to send her to school, and now she can't get a job. We figured a major like communications pretty much guaranteed she'd find work after college." She was thinking of her own experience when she had graduated from college—in 1983. That was then.

"As far as I'm concerned, Teresa did everything her father and I told her to do. She consulted the college's career counselors and read a few books about how to get a job. She created her résumé and wrote a cover letter—I know, I edited both—and started responding to job posts on Monster.com as well as a variety of corporate sites. She was very clear about what she wanted to do and initially stayed focused on positions that reflected her interests. After a month or so, when she didn't hear back from anyone, she started applying for anything just to get a job. Still nothing. The whole experience has been terribly frustrating."

Lisa's frustration is not unique. Many of you have been raised to believe that you can be anything you want. As it turns out, that's not necessarily true. This is creating angst for parents who feel responsible when you can't find jobs. On top of that is the unexpected financial burden. Many parents are spending as much as ten percent of their annual incomes on adult children who can't find jobs.

The rules your parents applied to their own job search are no longer relevant.

For instance, in 1983, the year Lisa graduated from college, Ronald Reagan was president, the economy was emerging from a recession, and unemployment, which peaked at 10.8 percent in 1982, was below 9 percent. By the end of the decade, unemployment was at less than 6 percent. By the mid-1980s private sector hiring was robust. American students still had little competition from foreign workers. Lisa heard from virtually everyone to whom she sent her résumé and received several excellent offers in the career she'd chosen.

"One thing's for certain," Lisa told me. "The way I got a job thirty years ago sure doesn't work today." She's right. When Lisa graduated, there were plenty of available jobs in America, and most went to American workers.

It is no wonder parents are frustrated. Today one in five of you who are in your twenties and early thirties still live with your parents. Over fifty percent of you receive financial support. When your parents were the same age, moving home for extended periods and getting financial support was almost unheard of.

It's easy to blame the usual suspects for the fact that so many of you are jobless - or underemployed - still living at home, and continuing to use your parents as your personal ATM. *The economy is lousy! You are lazy!* Interestingly there doesn't yet seem to be a lot of criticism aimed at colleges, very few of which include meaningful life-skills training in their curricula.

Whatever or whomever we might blame for the current employment conundrum there are forces at work that have forever altered the reality of job competition for recent college graduates. Regrettably we have been slow to grasp these realities and slower still to react. In a world where change is constant, the rate of change we've experienced in the last thirty years has been unprecedented.

The recession of 2008 has ended. Employment is back to prerecession levels, but recent graduates are still having trouble finding the kinds of jobs their education and skills suggest they should be getting. Assuming the recent recession was the sole reason for the high rate of unemployment for recent college graduates ignores significant realities that together have forever altered the labor picture.

There were plenty of signs indicating the American job market was in for a shock. Most of us ignored them. The reality arrived so quickly, most Americans were left wondering what hit them; hence the rush to place the entire blame on a weak economy. Four interconnected forces— a surge in competitors combined with the global education explosion, the technology revolution, and universally accessible information— were the real culprits. They still are. At the core these four forces, which emerged in the late twentieth century, resulted in remarkable changes in the world's economic balance, forever changing global economic and employment realities.

Pretending that our historical economic hegemony renders us somehow immune to competition puts us in considerable peril. It's time to confront the reality that we are in the middle of what historians will someday call a period of seismic change, in which these four powerful, interconnected forces merged to change history. As with all change, we can fight it and refuse to adapt to the inevitable. Conversely we can accept change, adapt to it, and discover the opportunities it creates.

The Surge in Competitors

In 1978, China's leaders took tentative steps toward developing a market system. At the time China barely warranted a footnote in the *World Economic Fact Book*. The seven Soviet-controlled Eastern European countries threw off the shackles of totalitarianism in 1991, and two years later the Soviet Union disintegrated, creating fifteen new nations. As most Americans saw it, the United States won the Cold War, and capitalism was breaking out all over the world. Middle classes were created; the newly wealthy became the new global consumer, and jobs were created to meet the demand.

What should be obvious is that many of the economies that were not particularly important to us thirty years ago are now major players on the world stage. The economic balance of power has been turned on its head. China, India, Indonesia, Brazil, Russia, Poland, and other Eastern European counties all have economies that have grown dramatically during the last thirty years. Today they provide goods, services, and human capital around the world, including in the United States. The so-called emerging markets represent more than 50 percent of world GDP.

As industry expands globally, more skilled workers are needed; training them requires improved education. As more skilled workers entered the workforce and earned market wages, they spent, resulting in a wave of global consumerism. The meteoric demand in goods and services meant cheaper labor could produce wanted goods, which in the past were manufactured at higher costs in the United States. Jobs went overseas at the same time that well-educated individuals, many educated at American colleges and universities, came to this country for higher paying jobs. "Made in America" still has global cachet value but it no longer means that an American made the item.

The Global Education Explosion

Since President Roosevelt signed the GI Bill into law, parents have viewed college as the ticket to a good job and a promising future. While college has never carried with it a promise of jobs after graduation, the fact that most students found jobs made it seem like a de facto guarantee. Competition for jobs has changed dramatically in the last five years, meaning that while a diploma is important, it does not by itself provide the competitive edge it once did.

In the past American students were competing with students just like them from schools all over the country for jobs after graduation. Today's competition is global, with well-educated students from China, India, and many other countries adding millions of highly qualified competitors to the labor pool every year. All of a sudden, the face of competition has changed; more available talent is chasing fewer jobs. Between 1993 and 2013, the US population grew by 22 percent. At the same time, the world population grew at a rate of 31 percent. Said another way, as the United States ages both figuratively and factually, developing parts of the world are educating more smart kids than we have kids.

Economists know that with more and better education, the per capita GDP of a country increases. It is no wonder, then, that countries like China and India are spending more each year on improving national education. It is an investment with a virtually guaranteed return.

The point is that in an era of greater connectivity, the pool of well-educated, talented labor has exploded. In this period of globalization, if you have skills and bring real value to an organization at a lower cost, it makes little difference in which country you reside. In today's flatter world, talent is fungible.

The Technology Revolution

Technological innovation has changed our concept of time. The speed of innovation means we are training students today using technologies that might well be obsolete by the time they graduate from college.

The rapid growth of efficient, laborsaving devices creates some jobs while making many more obsolete. Machines perform jobs in less time and at lower marginal costs than humans; they are capable of working 24/7 and don't need coffee breaks, vacations, or sick days. Technology is increasing competition in an already crowded field.

In 1978 Dr. Iben Browning predicted that technology would change the world. He was right; the proof is in our use of personal computers. For most of the twentieth century, computers were too large and too expensive for the average consumer; the Internet wasn't yet a place, and cyberspace wasn't even a word. Computers were slow by today's standards and functionally limited. All that has changed. There are more than 1.5 billion personal computers and 1.50 billion smartphones in use today.

It's not just the explosive development of laborsaving devices that has changed the employment picture. Technology has also helped lead the growth in education in many developing nations. For instance, India graduates more than 850,000 IT-trained students each year, creating skilled workers and opportunities for organizations in other countries to outsource IT jobs to that country.

It's useless to dwell on how outsourcing became a reality. We do need to embrace it as a fact of life and figure out how to work with it.

Universally Accessible Information

Information is power. One person with information and a smartphone has the power to share information with thousands with the click of a button. Now, that's power!

In 1990 the Internet was in its infancy; today it has leveled the global playing field by providing instant access to information to billions of people who are in turn becoming politically, socially, educationally, and economically enfranchised. There are almost fifty thousand Google searches performed every second of every day. That's six billion searches a day, or a staggering 2.2 trillion searches a year.

Facebook, which was founded in 2004, has 1.3 billion active monthly users, of whom 802 million are active daily users. Facebook on mobile devices is used almost 610 million times a day. Three hundred fifty million photos are uploaded to the site each day, and more than 3.2 billion "likes" and comments are posted daily.

Mobile devices are so efficient and universally connected that it's possible to call New York from atop Mount Kilimanjaro. Connectivity makes it possible to access Google in computer cafés in places that didn't even have cafés twenty years ago. All people on the globe can access the same information as long as they have the tools to do so. The bottom line is that an office is any place a cell phone can connect to the Internet.

Information is power, and universal, instantaneous access to information makes hundreds of millions of individuals who didn't have access ten years ago potential players in the global workplace. Further, the workplace has changed. It's no longer a cubicle you sit in, toiling at a job from nine to five. That world is as extinct as the dinosaurs.

New Realities

The surge in competitors, driven by education, technology, and universal access to information, has created a new world, one to which we have been slow to adapt.

You can't afford to delay your job search until the second semester of your senior year. The path to a career is a marathon, not a sprint. The process has to begin in high school.

The world today is different than it was when your parents were beginning their careers. Emerging technologies, the global education explosion, the technology revolution, and universally accessible information are all realities that have created an irreversible paradigm shift. That is, being American is no longer a guarantor of the American dream.

The Bottom Line

- Parents are spending as much as 10% of their annual income supporting adult children who can't find jobs.
- Over 50% of recent college graduates receive some sort of financial support from their parents.
- Today, one in five of you, in your twenties and early thirties, still live at home.
- The methods your parents applied to their job search are no longer relevant.
- Four interconnected forces - the New Realities - are behind the change, and they are;
  - Global Surge of Competition
  - Global Education Explosion
  - The Technology Revolution
  - Universally Accessible Information
- Moving home for an extended stay after graduation is not the road to independence.
- The path to a career is a marathon, not a sprint.
- The process has to begin in high school.

CHAPTER 4
The Generation Thing

Presidential elections are great theater, or sometimes, as the recent past suggests, theater of the absurd. They resemble slapstick comedy more than a serious exchange of constructive ideas. Debates resemble the dinner table scene in *The Nutty Professor*, each member of the family trying to out-fart the other. The process might be funny if the inability of the current ruling generation to focus on serious problems wasn't leaving you with a mess that you'll have to clean up.

It's not like cleaning up after the party your parents told you not to have when they trusted you to take care of the house while they went to Vegas for the weekend. Unfortunately, tackling global conflict, climate change, and global wealth imbalance makes removing beer stains from the heirloom Persian carpet seem like a walk in the park.

If you are going to scrub the mess the ruling generation is brewing, you first need to take control of your own destiny.

Start now, not after you graduate from high school or college. You want to start now because as far as preparing for the game of life is concerned, too many of you are being dealt a very bad hand.

My views on the way you are being raised are tainted by my own experiences as a student during the 1960s. It seems inevitable that as we age we acquire a curmudgeonly edge; grow less patient with youthful foibles. It is a kind of intergenerational sport to wax critically on the younger generation. You are so often lamented as lazy, slothful, unfocused, and irresponsible by your parents that many of you have started to believe it. Don't believe it; it's not true.

⸺⧟⸺

I once listened as a parent told me that today's students, including his own children, are lazy and unfocused. It's an opinion shared by many of the parents I met in seven years of teaching. While you appear to be unfocused at times, it is hardly your fault. Most of you are too busy trying to complete hours of homework, playing travel sports in addition to the sports you play at school, or taking cram courses so you can raise their SAT and ACT scores just enough to get into the *right* colleges. You are so busy bouncing from one parent-initiated activity to another that you have little time to focus.

Focus happens when you are engaged in something you really enjoy.

If you've experienced the feeling you get when you are "in the zone" you know what I mean. Sir Ken Robinson calls it the "element"—that feeling we get when our passions intersect with our skills. It is from that space that great ideas and accomplishments arise. We do our best thinking and best work when we are engaged in the zone. Passions can't be imposed. You need time and the support of your parents to find your true passions

Every generation is unique, branded by popular culture, crisis, changes in technology and more. That's not to say that one is better than the other, although through the filter of previous generations, the good old days are always yesterday. My parents were born and raised in an America that no longer existed by the time I arrived. The world in which they came of age was vastly different than mine. They no doubt wished mine were more like theirs.

I was born four years, two months and five days after my father, a lieutenant with the 76th Infantry Division, led E Company's last patrol the night before the war in Europe ended. In forty-five days of combat he was wounded twice and awarded two Bronze Star medals for valor.

Two days after VE Day, my mother, a Red Cross volunteer attached to the 9th Air Force, 386th Bomb Group, drove through Germany with her lover, an Air Force officer. They crossed the Rhine River on a pontoon bridge at Remagen, drove through Germany and into Czechoslovakia, stopping at the Carlsberg River: the Russian Army was on the other side.

My parents came of age during an extraordinary time in our history. Teens during the depression; their lives were indelibly marked by world economic crisis and World War II. The Great Depression made them appreciate stability, thrift and family security, while war gave then a special sort of pride in America. Emerging from both they wanted little more than prosperity, and peace and tranquility at home.

I am proud that my parents participated in seismic events. I also recognize that their lives were no more remarkable than the lives of millions of Americans who, as part of that generation, gave so much of themselves. Was Tom Brokaw guilty of hyperbole when he called them the Greatest Generation? I don't think so. Every generation of Americans has struggled to build on, improve, and defend the noble American experiment. But there was something remarkable about an entire generation rising to defend, not only our way of life, but also that of peoples in every corner of the globe.

When World War Two ended, millions of men and women came home, married, and started families. After more than a decade of declining birth rates, they rediscovered sex and made babies with unprecedented fervor. The result was a population bulge, passing through society like a pig through a python, inexorably moving and affecting everything in its path. The sixty million of us born between 1946 and 1964 were destined to be game changers.

Raised in the shadow of the Greatest Generation, many of us were conflicted. On one hand we felt enormous pride in what our parents had done. On the other hand we felt the ethos their experiences created was stifling and unreasonable. It was in fact, the basis of the generational war we waged in the 1960s.

When I was fourteen, my mother stuck her finger in my chest and said, "I just hope I live long enough to be a burden to you." It was perhaps the perfect tag line for intergenerational conflict.

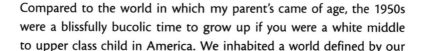

Compared to the world in which my parent's came of age, the 1950s were a blissfully bucolic time to grow up if you were a white middle to upper class child in America. We inhabited a world defined by our immediate neighborhoods. Mothers didn't work; when not in school we spent most of our time playing outdoors under their unseen but constant supervision. We weren't entertained; we invented games as needed and made up rules as we played. Childhood revolved around creativity and the ability to entertain ourselves.

We became the most, and best educated, generation in American history. Prior to the Servicemen's Readjustment Act, better known as the GI Bill, which was signed into law in 1944, higher education was not an option for most Americans. With the stroke of a pen, President Roosevelt had made education an entitlement for millions of American's, unwittingly contributing to the generational angst of the 1960s.

Education teaches us to question, to push back against ideas that don't make sense.

The Greatest Generation, the majority of whom did not attend college, was not comfortable with this new, better-educated generation, questioning the wisdom of doing things because it was the way it had always been done.

By the late 1950s the decade had become stale. In 1960 an underwhelming majority chose John Kennedy to lead us into the new decade. Kennedy's election was transformative. America was optimistic as the drab sameness of the 1950s was replaced by a vibrant new era. Young Americans were enthusiastically caught up in the spirit. We embraced Kennedy's call to serve: "Ask not what your country can do for you; ask what you can do for your country." Young Americans got involved.

The mood in America in the early 1960s was buoyant. Never mind that the seeds of a major war were being sown in a land that few could find on a map and the nuclear arms race nearly crescendoed in an apoc-alyptic exchange over an impoverished island 90 miles off our coast.

Friday, November 22, 1963 was the day that television news came of age. I was fourteen and smoking a cigarette behind the school gym when I heard that President Kennedy had been assassinated. For four days regular activities were suspended as we sat transfixed in front of our black and white television sets. Live television made us witnesses to the tragic pageantry of the funeral, and the murder of Lee Oswald by Jack Ruby.

Kennedy's assassination ushered in changes in the mood of the country. The first wave of Boomers was in college as Vietnam began to dominate the evening news. Students increasingly questioned our involvement in a war half way around the world against a country that posed little threat to the United States. They took up the cause of peace, racial equality and women's issues. In 1964 Bob Dylan released The Times They Are A Changin' -- As the present now will later be past -- the order is rapidly fading. Dylan proved to be prescient.

In 1966, Time Magazine selected an entire generation, our generation, as its man of the year. Called The Inheritor, we were "...a generation: the man – and woman – of 25 and under." According to Time, a generation had never been so assertive or so articulate or so well educated or so worldly. We were highly independent and that made our parents uncomfortable. They sensed that independence made us unpredictable and they were correct. The essay, as remarkable to read to today as it was in 1967, captured the essence of the generational struggle. Our struggle was a clash of ideologies - Vietnam, women's equality, race, and other contentious issues that defined the '60's.

The best-educated generation in the history of mankind was coming of age and we were not aging according to our parents' model. What ensued was a frighteningly unsettled era in which students pushed back, often violently, against the dictates of the current ruling generation. The times really were changing.

———— ∞∞∞ ————

Don't mistake this as a lecture by one more old fart, wallowing in memories of how good the good old days were and how, by comparison you are somehow deficient.

I don't believe you're deficient. Nor do I believe your generation is lazy, unfocused, over-indulged, self-indulged, or any other pejorative that has been attached by many of today's self-important pundits.

But I do believe you have an immediate hurdle you need to conquer before your talents can be channeled in directions that can measurably improve the state of the world we inhabit.

Throughout history, the United States has survived threats and setbacks to become the envy of the world community. The eclectic mix of malcontents and misfits who populated our shores created the spirit that made the twentieth-century the American Century. It wasn't easy. Through a combination of ingenuity, trial and error, risk, and courage, they made the American dream a reality. But today our country has a problem that threatens the foundation upon which it was built.

Some suggest, not for the first time, that our position in the world community is under assault, that the twenty-first century will be the Asian Century. In the late 1970s, pundits predicted that Japan would replace the United States as the world's great economy. While warning us that the sky was falling, the naysayers failed to take into account the competitive spirit that is built into the DNA of the American people.

We emerged from the dismal '70s, and reinvented ourselves. Bill Gates, Steve Jobs, and other visionaries, changed the way we live and think. Their vision changed the world. Now, in order to maintain our position in the global community, we need more of that entrepreneurial spirit.

Therein lies the problem. Before you can accomplish the great tasks that will ultimately define your generation, you need to reclaim your future.

Many parents are somehow convinced that you need to be micromanaged. You don't. They believe the world is more dangerous now than it was when they were your age. If anything, it's safer. But in believing it is more dangerous, parents have made "risk" a four-letter word. Without risk there is no discovery.

You need to be free to discover your interests and your talent.

You are tomorrow's leaders, but too few of you are receiving the training you need to solve the problems you will encounter in the future. Your parents fail you if they don't teach you how to identify and obtain positions in careers that best suit your strengths and interests. When you are engaged in activities that represent the intersection of your skills and passions, you are most apt to be creative, solve big problems, or foment lasting, positive change.

You should be learning decision-making, independence, the importance of failure, and ways to bounce back from failure. Learn how to fix your own problems. Unless you accept risk and failure as necessary to progress, you will be ill prepared to solve the problems you will inherit.

Parents with whom I speak say they want you to find your own passions and live happy, productive lives. Yet they overschedule you, cramming every available time slot with activities. It seems that every activity is designed to get you into the right college, so you can get the right job. But right for whom and by what standard? Unfortunately you are so busy, you have little time to yourself to discover your own future.

By depriving you of opportunities to use your imagination, discover your passions, make decisions, and learn accountability for your own mistakes, your future is being hamstrung.

While part of the problem lies with helicopter parenting it's not entirely your parents' fault. Instant connectivity makes it easy for you to call home every time you hit a snag instead of working through the problem yourself. Every time you do so you reinforce the notion that you are not yet ready for independence.

⸺ ◦∞◦ ⸺

If you want the future you deserve, take the initiative. Assert yourself. Engage your parents in different ways; illustrate through your actions that you are capable, dependable and ready to learn the important skills you will need in the future.

Start by having a conversation with your parents about tweaking the parent-child dynamic. Convince your parents to be your allies in a mission. You recognize that there are very big challenges in your future and you need their help. You want your parents to prepare you for the day when you are called on to solve them. You want them to mentor you; help you develop the skills that are essential to effective leadership and problem solving.

> *Change is difficult. Convincing your parents to change will not be easy.*

For starters, don't argue; arguing is counter productive and causes unnecessary tension. You might enlist your parents by asking for advice and counsel as you strive to identify your future role. *I need your help. Trust me... work with me... help me... be my ally. I might decide to work for the family business but I need to explore my options. If you decide my future for me I might miss my true calling.*

You want to communicate five critical messages.

1. **The Future Is About Me** - It is said that the future is about the young even though it often seems that you are being steered into a future you don't want. You want your parents to bury the urge to tell you that they want you to take over the family business or go to law school or be a doctor or anything else for that matter. Instead, you want them introduce you to the world of opportunities. If they do, you increase your chances of discovering what really interests you. Remember - you are most successful when you are interested and engaged.

2. **I Don't Need To Be Micromanaged** - You want strong leadership that supports you as you learn. Micromanaging is not leading, teaching, or, effective management. Micromanaging communicates a lack of confidence in your abilities, or even distrust. It inhibits personal development, and retard progress.

3. **I Want To Make Life a Laboratory** - As a teacher I was amazed by how many of my students were discouraged from pursuing opportunities to explore personal interests. Think of school as the petri dish for your future; your opportunity to explore subjects that are, or you think might, be of interest to you.

4. **I Can Do It** - Effective leaders see greater value in clearly defined guidelines than in the rigidity of rules, which by definition offer little room for exploration or interpretation. They know that nurturing an environment that places a premium on creativity and critical thinking is a time-honored way to identify talent. If you are given a task and clearly established guidelines, you

will learn by doing. Try to work through difficult problems on your own instead of looking for help too quickly. Growing up is experiential; you will learn by doing, trying new things, and making mistakes.

Having the responsibility to make your own decisions within the framework of clearly defined guidelines allows you to earn trust and greater amounts of responsibility. You gain confidence in your abilities. Don't worry about making mistakes. Making mistakes, and figuring out how to fix them on your own are important steps in the learning process.

5. **Trust Me and Empower Me: Build My Confidence - My first mentor was a remarkable man. He was one of the most effective leaders I've ever known. As a teacher and coach, his greatest contribution was the gift of confidence. He taught us the basics and developed game plans, but empowered us to take initiative on our own. This removed the stress of being wrong. That's what empowerment is all about.**

If you approach this in a business like way, your parents will be receptive. Remember, you are enlisting them as allies instead of engaging them in a no win argument. Put another way, you are proving that you are adult enough to find answers to difficult questions by focusing on a goal and assembling a support team to help you succeed.

This is not as radical as it sounds; it's the way most of your parents were raised. Given the opportunity, you will demonstrate that you are serious about your future and willing to do what is necessary prepare for success. You are expressing a desire to learn experientially. Your parents understand - they just need to be reminded - that empowerment and confidence go hand in hand as forces that drive success. They will be impressed that you grasp the importance.

The bottom line is this; you want your parents to be copilots on a journey, allies in pursuit of a common goal -- the future that best suits you.

Try it; you have nothing to lose. After all, it's your future we're talking about.

The Bottom Line

- If you are going to scrub the mess the ruling generation is brewing, you first need to take control of your own destiny.
- We do our best and most creative work when engaged in pursuits in which we have a genuine talent and are genuinely interested.
- Before you can accomplish the great tasks that will ultimately define your generation, you need to reclaim your future.
- Explore. Discover your interests.
- Learn decision-making, the role of failure, and ways to bounce back from failure.
- Embrace independence.
- Fix your own problems.
- Enlist your parents as mentors.
- You need advice and counsel as you strive to identify your future role.
- Tell your parents: *I need your help. Trust me, work with me, and be my ally. I need to explore my options. If you decide my future for me I might miss my true calling.*
- Communicate five critical messages to your parents:
  - The Future Is About Me
  - I Don't Need To Be Micromanaged
  - I Want My Life To Be A Laboratory
  - I Can Do It
  - Trust Me and Empower Me: Build My Confidence
- It's your future - take charge.

CHAPTER 5
What Happened To Us?

*N*ever *trust anyone over thirty. Question authority.*
When I was a student it seemed that there were too many old people, making too many rules. The Boomers pushed back hard – we were nothing if not confrontational.

Then we graduated from college, got jobs, and learned that questioning authority was the quick way to the unemployment line. When we turned thirty we decided we were trustworthy. When authority was in our hands, power gave us amnesia. We made rules — lots of rules.

Parents love rules. Some rules make sense: others don't. I suspect I imposed a few rules for no other reason than I could. Power corrupts. You live with more rules and less freedom of choice than we had.

If parents love rules, many hate risk. Those who do are reluctant to embrace trial and error as a learning tool. That's a problem. More rules and less freedom of choice inevitably result in risk aversion.

Risk, calculated risk, is essential to the development of effective problem solvers, innovators,

entrepreneurs and leaders. Over protecting is dumbing down the process of growing up.

Micromanagement has gone to extreme limits under the guise of keeping you safe. Some of my former students who are now in college tell me their parents monitor them by putting GPS tracking applications on their cell phones. I don't know about you, but as far as I'm concerned that's not parenting; that's stalking.

Naturally not all students mature equally. But most of the ones I taught had a wealth of talent and knowledge that eclipsed those of their parents when they were the same age. Most were mature enough to assume increasing levels of decision-making authority if given the opportunity.

That said while you have so many positive attributes, you seem to lack the confidence you need in order to translate skills into action. Many of you seem to have trouble connecting the dots—understanding how to use what you know to solve complex problems. If you want freedom you have to prove you can handle it. Regrettably, your parents are slow to give you the opportunity.

There is no better time than high school for your parents to start letting go. That means surrendering control. Mike Myatt, chief strategy officer at N2growth, says that great leadership means surrendering responsibility. Myatt's advice is no less important for your parents than it is for CEOs.

According to Myatt, "...the words leadership and surrender are rarely used together in complementary fashion. Society has labeled surrender as a sign of leadership weakness, when in fact it can be among the greatest of leadership strengths. He says that effective leaders learn the ever so subtle art of letting go."

You want your parents to lengthen the leash. Sharing control signals confidence in your ability, which in turn boosts your self-confidence. So to answer the question of when, now is not too soon. But remember, trust is both given and earned, and every action, good or bad, has a consequence.

Increased freedom carries with it increased accountability. That's the all-important trade-off.

Accept this reality: no one but you can make you successful.

Your parents can create an environment that enhances the possibility of success; the desire and drive to achieve great things come from within.

In her book *Slouching Toward Adulthood*, Sally Koslow suggests your generation is more coddled than any previous generation. You are risk averse, reluctant to make waves, and woefully unaware of the state of the world you stand to inherit. We need you capable of making informed decisions, fighting your own battles, fixing screwups, and taking responsibility for your actions.

When you are over-managed, overindulged, and over-pampered, barriers form between between you and your ultimate success. Despite what you have been led to believe, you don't need the pampering. You are a remarkably resourceful generation. Overprotecting, overindulging, and over-managing risks create a sense of entitlement while depriving you of valuable experience that comes from making decisions and solving problems yourselves.

You are capable of more independence and less parental oversight than you currently have, according to Madeline Levine, a practicing psychologist in Marin County, California. Levine wrote in the *New York Times*, "...if parents treat your walking toddler as if she can't walk, you diminish her confidence and distort reality. Ditto nightly 'reviews' of homework, repetitive phone calls 'just to check if you're OK' and 'editing' (read: writing) your child's college application essay."

Ultimately your success depends on your ability to stand up for yourself. It is axiomatic that risk accompanies greater amounts of autonomy and risk comes with consequences.

When I was twelve my cousin and I were shooting BB guns in a field behind his house. I screwed up and shot a pellet into my right index finger. My mother didn't pull any punches: *How did you manage to do something so stupid?*

Okay. I screwed up, as no one hesitated to tell me. My parents didn't get angry, although I suspect they were relieved that the injury was minor. They assumed I'd learn from my mistake, period — end of story. Nobody called a lawyer, threatened to sue Daisy Rifles, or my cousins, or anyone else.

Five months later I was given a 22 rifle for Christmas. I'd learned my lesson and my parents knew it. Experience is a great teacher. I never made the mistake again.

Don't get me wrong, I'm not advocating for guns. The last thing we need is to put more firepower in the hands of untrained American gun nuts. Back when my friends and I were armed to the teeth with Daisy BB guns and Winchester 22 caliber rifles, we were trained by a generation of men who were paid to shoot at people who were paid to shoot back at them.

I once told the mother of one of my students about the trip I took to Europe in 1970, the summer after my sophomore year in college. "My daughter wants to do the same thing, but I won't let her," she said. "You know, the world is much more dangerous now."

Really? Your grandfather was dodging flack over Berlin, or landing on Omaha Beach when he was barely out of his teens. Your father came of age in the Cold War. Don't forget the Cuban Missile Crisis, polio and that little dust-up in Vietnam. Sure, terrorists, ISIS, and Hezbollah are dangerous; so is crossing the street. Every era has its dangers. Are those dangers greater than the ones we faced a generation ago? I don't think so.

To be fair the world *is* different now than it was in 1970. But that doesn't mean the potential risks are greater — different maybe, but not greater. To be deprived of an experience because the world is a dangerous place limits learning, options and opportunity.

We were expected to learn by trying. We failed as we learned. Some of life's best lessons are learned when one fails. Failure helps you find your boundaries; what you are really capable of.

Sometimes I wonder if we're raising the first generation of American citizens to run away from a good challenge. Be careful. That's risky. Let me do it for you. Life is risky business *so you better learn how to deal with it yourself — the sooner the better.*

One day I was walking with Charlie, my golden retriever, when we met Isabelle, a young Swedish woman who was in Princeton visiting her mother. As we talked, Isabelle told me she had graduated from high school and was taking a gap year before beginning her university studies. Immediately after graduating, she and a classmate traveled for five months throughout Australia, New Zealand, Bali, and Thailand. Isabelle and her friend, both eighteen years old at the time, were on their own. They relied on their confidence, abilities, and passion for discovery to make the trip a success. They didn't sign on to any kind of tour and kept their itinerary as flexible as possible. For the most part, they found lodging as needed.

I decided my students should meet Isabelle, an individual their own age who had stepped out of her comfort zone to explore the world of possibilities. Delighted to have the opportunity to visit an American classroom, Isabelle agreed to speak with the class.

The students' reactions to her story were predictable: they were amazed. "You mean your parents let you do that?" "Didn't you worry about falling behind if you took a gap year? How did you know how to plan a trip like that?" "What happened if you ran into problems?"

To my surprise Brad, an outstanding athlete and the oldest student in the class, offered that he could "never do anything like that."

"Why not?"

"I wouldn't even know where to begin. I mean, how did you know what you were doing and where you were going to stay and stuff like that? I guess your parents must have done a lot of that for you. Right?"

"No. The trip was my idea and my responsibility. No one offered to help, and I never thought to ask. I just did the research and put the trip together."

Isabelle's response to Brad's question led to a spirited conversation. Many of his classmates agreed with his comments. Several students weighed in, saying their parents would never let them travel on their own, without an agenda, even if they were in college. A couple said their parents wouldn't allow it even after they graduated!

Wow!

Push back when someone tells you that what you want to do is too difficult or too risky. If you hear it enough you'll begin to believe it, or worse, begin to doubt yourself.

You were born with an innate determination to succeed. You pushed through hardship, pain, and mind-numbing frustration just learning to walk. You failed time after time; the process must have seemed an eternity. But you didn't give up. Walking on all fours like the family dog was not an option. Finally you succeeded.

Success was yours and yours alone. No one could speed the process, ease the frustration, or eliminate the risk of injury. You got encouragement when you needed it. You were smothered in atta girls. Success needs cheerleaders. But over time cheerleading became something different.

Parents seem to believe that you need them more than you do. They often confuse bulldozing with mentoring; in the long run this works against you.

By hovering, over-protecting, fighting your battles and doing for you what you can do your-selves, parents put the brakes on the independence process.

Figure things out. Take charge. Fix your own mistakes when you make them. Take a few risks. If you don't like something the way it is, change it. Don't look for someone to do it for you. The biggest impediment to your success is you. Get out of your comfort zone and try new things.

Don't be afraid to try and don't be discouraged if success takes time. Things don't always go according to plan. Shit happens — you're going to screw up. Your parents did. You will too.

Mistakes and failures are not only inevitable they're necessary. As Einstein said, "Anyone who has never made a mistake has never tried anything new."

Hiring managers are looking for critical thinkers and problem solvers. They want employees who are agile and adaptable. Curiosity and imagination are coveted traits.

Don't let your parent's good intentions make you less valuable to a potential employer.

You are a lot more capable than you think. Take charge – do it yourself.

The Bottom Line

- Parents love rules. Some rules make sense, others don't.
- You have many positive attributes, but too many of you seem to lack the confidence needed to translate skills into action.
- You are a remarkably resourceful generation. You don't need pampering, over-protecting, or over-indulging.
- Shared control helps you build confidence in your abilities.
- Increase freedom carries increased responsibility.
- Ultimately your success depends on your ability to stand up for yourself.
- Failure helps you find boundaries; what you are really capable of.
- Take ownership of your mistakes. Whenever possible fix them your self.
- Don't be afraid to try and don't be discouraged if success takes time.
- Shit happens. Things don't always go according to plan.
- You are more capable than you think.
- If you don't like something the way it is, change it.
- Take charge - do it yourself.

CHAPTER 6
Parents Are Dazed And Confused

The ruling generation always seems to be stuck in the past. *That's the way it's always been done.* There is rarely room for debate. The more you try to reason, explain or argue that times might have changed, the less prepared they think you are to handle life on your own. You're not the only generation to suffer the epidemic of faux-expertise.

When I was a kid my father and I seemed to argue about everything: hair length, Vietnam, curfews, music and race. Reflecting on our arguments I recall that at times I tried using logic to prove a point. Once when he was in the market for a new car, I suggested to my father that he consider a Japanese automobile. "I'll never buy a car from those people," he said. "Not after what they did during the war." If that's the case, I wanted to know, why is that all of our television sets were made in Japan? Somehow, the logic of that question proved only the depth of my stupidity.

Many parents are confused by two taxing realities: generational differences, and a new or redefined endgame. Instead of embracing change and learning how to work with new realities, their response is to tighten their control.

Believe it or not, your generation, that seems to your parents to be drifting through life, struggling for identity, wedded to computer games and Facebook, and sleeping past noon is the one that will be deciding our fate in twenty or thirty years. If that's a scary thought to your parents, remember: it was to your parent's parents as well.

If your parents' job is to prepare you to assume the mantle of leadership in an era of constant change often, it often seems insurmountably difficult. Too often they apply yesterday's solutions to today's problems even though new problems require new solutions. As Joshua Cooper Ramo wrote in *The Age of the Unthinkable*, "We've left our future...in the hands of people whose greatest single characteristic is that they are bewildered by the present."

As leaders you will be called on to make critical decisions, to solve the problems for which we have not yet found solutions, or problems we have caused.

Expecting you to find solutions using the same processes that no longer work is a non-starter.

It's time to "think different." As Ramo said, "...in a revolutionary era of surprise and innovation, you need to learn to think and act like a revolutionary."

Sustainable change often begins by finding opportunity in adversity. There are tangible reasons for encouraging you to use your imagination. Relying on old formulas in new environments is stagnating.

Successful solutions to difficult problems require trial and error -- the willingness to accept the risk of failing. After all there is no guarantee that every decision you make will be a good one. As a friend—an entrepreneur all of his working life—said, "Successful entrepreneurs see opportunities others miss and then turn their visions into reality. That means experimenting with possibilities and being willing to be wrong more often than you are right."

Globalization, a shrinking middle class, and today's vastly different employment landscape make the inevitability of the American dream more uncertain today than at any time in the recent past.

Planning one's journey into the future requires a redrawing of the road map. As it will fall to you to deal with the weighty matters you inherit, you want to identify and pursue the future for which you are best suited. In *The Global Achievement Gap*, Tony Wagner identified seven skills hiring managers' value:

- Critical thinking and problem solving.
- Collaboration across networks and leading by influence.

- Agility and adaptability.
- Initiative and entrepreneurialism.
- Effective written and oral communications.
- Accessing and analyzing information.
- Curiosity and imagination.

Wagner is blunt. If parents and educators do not attend to these skills, he wrote, they "are putting their children at an increased risk of not being able to get and keep a good job, grow as learners, or make positive contributions to their communities."

The secret to success in the long run is identifying strengths and matching them with passions. Ken Robinson wrote in *The Element* that successful people find "high levels of achievement and personal satisfaction upon discovering the thing that they naturally do well and that also ignites their passions." Athletes talk of being in the zone, a place where training, physical ability, and the will to win meet. All distractions fade away; it's just a competitor and a goal. Great things happen when an individual is in his or her element or zone. The proper thing to do is help him or her find it.

While education is a critically important part of the puzzle, it is not the only part. You need mentors to provide advice and guidance while you try to make sense of what you are learning in school. You spend three quarters of the year in school. The time you spend often seems like an exercise in data dumping, absorbing stuff that does not seem particularly relevant. This is why mentors matter.

Mentoring is a supportive and inclusive process that requires collaboration. It is goal oriented, designed to create teamwork and unity of purpose.

Because mentoring focuses on the mentee, the "us versus them" conflict students often voice is significantly reduced. This is not to say mentors aren't disciplinarians. Effective mentors are honest and at times blunt. A mentor's job is to counsel, and a counselor who is not honest is not doing his or her job. Mentoring is teaching. It is also training, encouraging self-discovery and creativity, and illustrating that failing is not necessarily failure.

This is why you want your parents to embrace mentoring. Today the speed of change—driven by technological innovation and increased connectivity, the very forces that define your generation—often makes success seem elusive. Times have changed. Your parents should ground the helicopters; park the bulldozers, and stop hovering and over-managing. Those classic micromanagement techniques effectively stifle discovery, discourage risk, and are inherently counterproductive.

Leaders don't manage people to success; they lead them to it.

Mentoring is an essential element in effective leadership. Helicopter parenting on steroids à la Amy Chua, author of *Battle Hymn of the Tiger Mom*, will not prepare you to "think differently." Don't get me wrong, your parents need to be involved every step of the way. But by the time you are in high school, and certainly when you are in college, they can start flattening the hierarchical structure.

Admission to college is no longer the endgame it once was. Today the end game has shifted to landing a meaningful career after graduation. As recently as ten years ago, college graduates were confident of finding meaningful employment soon after graduation.

Not long ago your competitor was the student sitting next to you in your finance class. Today the available labor pool is global. Thirty years ago Americans dreamed of the end of the Cold War and a world without communism. We dreamed of capitalism breaking out in every corner of the globe. Beware the ancient curse: may you get what you wish for. Driven by a global capitalist movement, more and better education worldwide, new technologies, automation, and an expanded global workplace, the competition for jobs is very different now from what it once was.

Back in the day, when college acceptance letters arrived, parents could congratulate themselves on a job well done and start planning for life as empty nesters. Today, if they aren't adequately preparing you for the realities of post-college career competition, they had better keep the home lights burning. A growing number of unemployed graduates are moving back in with their parents after college—and they are staying for a long time.

You are going to be asked to tackle significant problems at home and around the world. This can be a daunting prospect if you don't know where you fit. Your parents have been slow to recognize that the career landscape has changed. Accepting this reality, your parents can be of genuine assistance.

Great things can happen when you and your parents collaborate. Top-down decisions breed reluctant followers, while collaboration creates partners with a common mission.

Nothing instills a sense of importance and responsibility like being asked to participate in the decision-making process.

Many of your parents ply their trade in corporate America. They understand the concept of including young, new hires in the decision making process; it's how talent is developed. Comparisons between families and businesses are clear, yet I have spoken with parents—some of whom are successful executives—who don't recognize that the steps they take to develop talent at work are will also work at home. Many parents compartmentalize their lives by leaving work at work. That's admirable, but everything that happens at work isn't a problem.

Corporations have sound reasons for including young employees in planning sessions. First, young minds not yet tainted by tradition are far less apt to begin conversations with "the way we've done it in the past..." In today's bottom-up world, successful leaders have trained themselves to listen for the "what if?" moment. Second, giving young employees opportunities to participate in the decision-making process is an integral component of mentoring; it's how successful corporations develop future leadership. They take mentoring extremely seriously for one simple reason: it works.

Truly successful corporations have processes in place to ensure that young employees are prepared for increasing amounts of responsibility. In order to stay competitive, corporate leaders must develop talent and sophisticated processes to mentor talent. Identifying and nurturing future leadership are part of succession planning, and they are key to the long-term success and survival of a corporation.

If mentoring works in the office, it makes sense that it should work at home. Your parents can prepare you for futures in which you will confidently step into leadership roles. The world that you are entering today is vastly different from that of ten years ago. Successful businesses stay at the top of their game by recognizing the inevitability and importance of change. Today the rate of change is accelerating faster than at any other time in history, which means we have a shorter runway to make the right decisions, and the consequences of our decisions are more critical than ever.

The Bottom Line

- Older generations often seem to be stuck in the past.
- Generational differences often lead to frustration.
- Leaders are change agents.
- Leaders don't manage people to success; they lead them to it.
- Mentoring is an essential element in effective leadership.
- Sustainable change often begins with finding opportunity in adversity.
- As leaders you will be called on to make critical decisions and solve difficult problems.
- Successful solutions often require trial and error.
- Identify your strengths and match them with your passions.
- Mentoring is supportive and inclusive.
- Mentoring requires collaboration.
- College is no longer the endgame it once was.
- The endgame is now finding a meaningful position in the career that you have determined is right for you.

CHAPTER 7
You Can Help

I f your parents are going to help you prepare for life after graduation they will need your help. They are confused and confusion has
resulted in non-productive over-involvement. Start with constructive
advice. Disabuse them of the notion that hovering and over-protecting
is helpful. By fighting your battles, preaching risk avoidance, telling you
what courses to take, and what college is right for you, your parents are
doing you more harm than good.

You want your parents to rethink the way they help you prepare
and that means radical changes in the parent-child dynamic. As counter-
intuitive as it will sound to them, by relaxing their hold, and lengthening
your leash, they are speeding the process by teaching you to think inde-
pendently. The weight of the evidence, measured by the dismal results
of recent graduates trying to find meaningful employment, suggests that
all of their hovering, overscheduling, cajoling, pushing, and imposing
strategies to make you successful doesn't work.

*Before anything can change,
everyone involved need to drop*

the illusion that your parents will make you successful.

They can set the stage, but your ultimate success exists in your desire and willingness to be successful. Setting the stage for success is a team effort.

Take, as an example, Roger Federer. Federer is one of the greatest tennis players in the history of the game. He has access to great coaches and superb trainers, and he puts in hours of practice. He also has an inner drive to succeed.

Federer is an extraordinary athlete; once he's at center court at Wimbledon, the moment is his. Whether he wins or loses depends on how well he competes against his adversary. At that point his coaches, his trainers, and all the people who helped him get there are merely spectators. But in the truest sense, his coaches and trainers are his partners—allies in his success. They share a common goal.

Federer's example illustrates the central theme of this book: your parents can be coaches, trainers, and cheerleaders, but they can't make you succeed. They can't even make you want to succeed. Federer is a champion because he wants to be a champion. He is willing to do what is necessary to be one. He plays tennis to fulfill his dream, not those of his parents. While they undoubtedly provided the tools and the space he needed to succeed, only Federer could make it happen.

Let me be clear: by suggesting that your parents back off, I am not saying they should disengage. To the contrary they need to be engaged for longer than ever before, but in different ways. If college is no longer a de facto guarantee of a job, it's important that your parents take an active role in helping you prepare for the challenge. Convince them to change the way they help. You want them to observe, listen, counsel, mentor, partner, and ally, instead of pushing, driving, and imposing. Ask your parents to engage differently, as allies, in ways that encourage you to be innovative, to find your passions and purposes in life.

—∞∞—

In this age of helicoptering and bulldozing, being engaged has become synonymous with overscheduling, overindulging, over-programming, and doing for you what you should be doing yourself. Your lives seem so programmed that it is a wonder you have any time to yourselves to figure out what you want to do in the future.

If your goal is to land a meaningful job in the career, the process has to begin at home while you are still in high school.

You want your parents to nurture creativity so you can discover your innate talents and interests. Using your initiative to solve problems on your own is important step toward self-discovery. You will make mistakes and occasionally fail. Shit happens - it's not the end of the world. To the contrary, failure is a great learning tool.

Somehow your parents and you have come to believe that you need them more than you actually do. Parents have confused bulldozing with mentoring, and in the long run this works against you.

Harnessing independence deprives you of important confidence-building opportunities. It is vitally important that you tackle problems on your own. In doing so you will discover strengths you don't realize you possess.

College is where you will hone skills like networking and interviewing; skills you will need to land the dream job in the career you want. But you need to be taught the skills before you get to college. For most of you, college is the first time you are truly on your own, living outside of daily parental scrutiny.

In *That Used to Be Us*, Thomas Friedman and Michael Mandelbaum wrote that today's employers are "looking for workers who can think critically, who can tackle non-routine complex tasks and who can work collaboratively with teams located in their office or globally." More often than not, the deciding factor in an interview will be your ability to communicate that you are innovative. Since the endgame is getting a job after graduation, it is important to start by building the skills employers find valuable.

Tony Wagner wrote in *Creating Innovators* that play leads to the discovery of passion, and passion becomes purpose. We've all had the experience of being involved in something and having so much fun, time is subordinated to passion. We do our best work when we get into that zone. If you want to enjoy a productive career doing what you love, you should encourage your parents to help you find your passions.

Knowing what you love to do, what you are good at, and what matters to you is remarkably empowering.

Maybe you've experienced the feeling you get when you are engaged in doing things about which you are passionate. You lose track of time. Your passion is reflected in your voice and body language. You enjoy a sense of purpose and confidence.

Your parents have dreams for you. They want you to lead happy, productive, and successful lives. Unfortunately what they often communicate is that they want you to be happy, productive, and successful living the life they imagine for you. The future belongs to you; the direction you take in life is more critical to our country's future than ever before.

The global problems you will be called on to solve are enormously complex. Your parent's job should be to help you find your niche, where you can be most productive to yourself and society. You can make a positive difference, but nobody ever made a difference by simply making a living.

Too many of you will graduate from college confused about your future. Many of you have no idea what you want to do with your lives. Some of you will pursue careers in which you have little interest because it's what your parents want you to do. You will be best prepared to find your place if you are empowered to find your own interests and talents.

Too many people pour out of elevators after work, day in and day out, their eyes locked in thousand-yard stares -- tacit admissions that they hate what they do. Too many are trapped in careers they don't enjoy because of decisions they made for the wrong reasons. You don't want that to happen to you.

You will thrive if you are raised in an environment in which you are given the opportunity to discover your interests, encouraged to visualize your future, and taught the skills you will need to turn your visions into realities.

But you can't do it alone.

A by-product of the changing career landscape is that many of your parents hyper-focus on increased competition for traditional jobs. They create an almost-manic drive to get you into the *right* school so that you can land the *right* career. Parents are far more involved in your lives than ever before. The nature of that involvement is hurting, not helping.

Have you ever noticed how children under five years old have remarkable abilities to find new passions? It seems everything they encounter is a marvel. They ask questions, try new things, probe, explore, and dare to fail. They deal with failure easily because they do not yet understand the concept as an absolute. They have an innate determination to succeed. Consider the determination, hardship, pain, and mind-numbing frustration you experienced when you learned to walk. You experienced failure after failure; the process must have seemed to take an eternity. But you did not give up. Walking on all fours like the family dog was not an option. You gutted it out until you succeeded.

Your parents can't walk for you. They can't speed the process, ease the frustration, or entirely eliminate the risk of injury. What they can do is encourage, give boosts when needed, and lavish praise for every success until you finally succeed. Over time, the concept of risk - failure - reward becomes a pejorative. The can-do spirit and zeal for discovery and innovation are replaced by risk aversion. In a sense, while trying to do what's best for you, parents are guilty of overtly or subliminally throwing water on creative fires. They say things like:

- "Be careful—that's dangerous!"
- "What can you do with a degree in Bosnian art history?"
- "I really hope you'll join me in the family business."
- "That's tricky. I'll take care of it for you."

School psychologist Dana Lieberman believes a shift begins in the seventh grade: "With upper school just a couple of years away, parents begin to shift their attention from learning the basics to grades, while at the same time teachers become much more focused on content. This is the point where college counselors advise what courses will be more attractive on a transcript and grades trump actual learning."

A colleague told me about an e-mail she received from a parent of a student to whom she had given a marking period grade that was lower than acceptable to the parent. The email read, "An eighty will look much better than a seventy-four, so you need to change my child's midterm grade." We have to wonder if it ever occurred to that parent to tell the kid she probably got what she deserved, and if she wanted a better grade, she might work a little harder.

The same student was a two-letter varsity athlete, a star on both the soccer and softball fields. Three times a week, after practice at school, she had evening practice with her travel teams—a forty-five minute drive each way. She frequently didn't begin her homework until after she finally got home and had dinner. However, teachers can't be expected to adjust their grading because a student is over-scheduled, and parents can't blame teachers when a student's grades suffer because she is exhausted. The student and her parents needed to prioritize.

Convince your parents to be your allies. Allying in pursuit of a common goal is powerful. When your parents ally with you, they help open doors to wonderful futures.

History is rich with examples of alliances that accomplished great things. From victory in World War II to putting a man on the moon, we have achieved goals that seemed too great for any one person or group to realize. For you, the life goals you want to achieve are no less important than putting a man on the moon. And they shouldn't be.

You have a goal. Now create a road map to arrive at your goal. This means breaking your ultimate goal into a series of smaller goals and leveraging allies' strengths by assigning them tasks that best reflect those strengths. While allies will disagree on tactics and argue about interim priorities, the process of disagreement and debate makes a stronger alliance—as long as everyone is focused on the endgame.

Allies rarely share all the same skill sets. Partners in an alliance have unique strengths and weaknesses. The purpose of joining forces is to leverage each other's strengths while providing support where needed. Allies grow together, resolve differences, and adapt to circumstances as they arise if the endgame is clear, desired by all, and mutually beneficial.

Being an ally with you does not mean your parents should do it—whatever "it" is—for you. Many people, including many of you, believe that you are lazy. If it is true, and I don't believe it is, it's because your parents are overly involved in your success. They do your chores, write your college essays, plan your trips and schedules, all of which you should be doing yourself.

> By doing for you what you should be doing for yourself, parents are inhibiting your growth.

Performing tasks for you that you can and should be doing yourself is not constructive. Allies work with each other in order to attain a common goal. They balance individual skills, teach, support, and offer constructive criticism.

If the goal is for you to land a meaningful job in the career you choose, your parents must agree that you should be encouraged to identify the jobs that are best for you. Their task is to create an environment that nurtures that goal.

Your parents are confused. You can help them focus on what is really important by convincing them to be your allies in pursuit of your life goals.

The Bottom Line

- Drop the illusion that your parents will make you successful.
- Your success exists in your desire and willingness to be successful.
- In this age of helicoptering and bulldozing, being engaged has become synonymous with overscheduling, overindulging, over-programming, and doing for you what you should be doing yourself.
- Using your initiative to solve problems on your own is an important step toward self-discovery.
- Restricting your independence deprives you of important confidence-building opportunities. It is vitally important that you tackle problems on your own. In doing so you will discover strengths you don't realize you possess.
- Failure is a learning tool.
- Networking and interviewing are critical skills: learn them at home - hone them in college.
- Build a strategic alliance with your parents.
- The purpose of working as allies is to leverage off of each other's strengths while providing support where necessary.
- Create goals and create a roadmap to arrive at your goal.
- Perform the tasks you can and should be doing yourself.
- The future belongs to you; the direction you take in life is more critical to our country's future than ever before.
- The global problems you will be called on to solve are enormously complex.
- Your parent's job should be to help you find your niche, where you can be most productive to yourself and society.
- You can make a positive difference, but nobody ever made a difference by simply making a living.

CHAPTER 8
Take Charge Of You

One evening, at dinner with friends, one of the women regaled us with a story about the time she got her first diaphragm. As the story goes, a nurse explained how one inserted a diaphragm, then stayed in the room as my friend tried, failing repeatedly, to grasp the art of diaphragm insertion. After several abortive attempts the nurse sighed, "Honey, I'll explain this to ya just one more time. Remember, I ain't gonna be there with ya when it happens, so ya gotta learn to do it yourself."

More recently, I sent a message to a friend, a former student who was in Italy for her semester abroad. I suggested that she visit Sienna, about an hour from Florence where she was studying. The town is an enchanting medieval gem: savory food, priceless art and stunning architecture. I received several questions in return: "How do I get there?" "What will I do?"

If the first story is funny, the second is troubling. Where's the sense of adventure, that can do spirit? Why not take a hands on approach: "I to do it, I'll figure it out." Reaching for help every time you encounter something new might make your life easier in the short run, but it is hurting you in the long run. Coddling is not what life is all about. You don't need it or want it.

Ask yourself two questions: Am I ready to assume greater responsibility for my actions? Am I comfortable with the consequences?

If you are honest with yourself you may find that the answer to both is "probably not." Don't worry. It's not entirely your fault; you've been raised to think you are entitled. You've been raised to believe that win, lose, or draw everyone gets a trophy.

Winning is not about showing up. Winning is about training, experiencing the sting of failure, and learning how to bounce back. Welcome challenge, stare down adversity, invite risk, balance options, fail and learning from it, pick yourself up, and look for the next potential failure.

Take charge now; don't wait. Set goals and create road maps to achieve your goals. You'll encounter problems along the way. So what? You are capable -- definitely not a wimp -- and will find a way to solve the problems. It's all part of the learning process; perfection is not reality. Fixing your problems teaches you ingenuity, and learning how to fight your own battles is an invaluable life skill.

Every generation faces challenges. The problems you will be called upon to resolve are immense, and your ability to do so will ultimately define your generation. There is no trophy for failure. If you really want something, you'll have to earn it. Brace yourself for disappointments, learn to deal constructively with failure, and above all stop asking everyone else to solve your problems.

If you want something, get it yourself. If you don't like something the way it is, change it; don't look around for someone to do it for you. Accepting that the biggest impediment to your success is you is a giant step toward a life well led.

Where do you begin? Find a passion, have a vision, make goals, and create a plan to achieve them so you can ultimately realize your vision. Identify your innate strengths, focusing on the things you enjoy.

Recognizing your strengths and acknowledging your weaknesses, allows you to take charge of the enormous reservoir of talent you possess.

Knowing your strengths and how you add value gives you leverage. You can meet big challenges by harnessing your talents. Self-awareness is incredibly empowering. Think of the big game, that critical test, or the time you addressed the entire student body. If you were up for the challenge, it was because you were prepared. Preparation gives you confidence, and confidence empowers.

Your future is about you. Any argument that you are too young to make a difference is spurious. Steve Jobs founded Apple when he was twenty-one. Now, twenty-eight years later, it is one of the most valuable companies in the world. Facebook founder Mark Zuckerberg is in his early thirties. Martin Luther King Jr. was only thirty-nine when he was assassinated; in those thirty-nine years he accomplished enough to fill several lifetimes.

That's not to say we can all be Jobs, Zuckerberg, or King, but you are all capable of making positive differences right now. Looking at the world he will inherit, a student said his generation needed to "take a step back, look at how it was done in the past, throw that shit out, and start anew." He might be right. Learn to question conventional wisdom. "If the old ways worked," he said, "then the old problems would be solved already."

Hiring managers increasingly take note of the valuable skills some students possess. Successful companies like Amazon, 3M, and IBM recognize that the rates of change in technology, discovery, and world events require young minds and new, creative thinking. This is why so many companies are creating flatter organizational structures and shifting to bottom-up leadership styles.

So what are you doing to get ready for your time when it comes? And what do you want to do? At the very least, by the time you leave home for college your focus should be on you. Remember: you might well live with the decisions you make today for a very long time. That alone should help you focus.

What you ultimately do with your life is your business. You can be a doctor or a pole dancer, a derivatives trader, a dietitian, or a surfer dude. The decision to choose a career in finance, law, medicine, the military, or the church should depend on what you want to do with your life— no more and no less.

Your parents might dream of the day you discover a genetic link between male pattern baldness and gerbils, but that does not have to be your dream. Nor does it have to be your life sentence.

Be perfectly clear on this: your parents cannot make you successful. They might make you rich. They can make you happy and sad and angry and glad; parental job descriptions require that they'll drive you crazy at times. They can do all those things and more, but always remember they can't make you successful. That part is up to you. What they can do is prepare you to be successful, and you should expect and demand that they do. Remember: success requires that you be ready for your opportunity when it comes!

The most import thing you can do right now is to begin building a team of personal advisors. These are your mentors, allies; the individuals to whom you can turn for advice or as sounding boards.

I was a sophomore in high school when an exceptional teacher taught me how good it feels like to succeed. An ADHD before much was known about the disorder, I was every teacher's worst nightmare come true. I'm sure most thought I was either stupid or remarkably lazy. As it turned out, I was neither. I had undiagnosed learning issues and struggled academically. The result was that I became conditioned to accept bad grades as my personal reality. For me, mediocrity became a self-fulfilling prophecy.

I took Robert Nicolls' American history class in my sophomore year. Mr. Nick, as we called him, cared deeply about his students. His powers of observation were remarkable. I was thrilled to take his class although true to form I was at best a C student. That changed the day Mr. Nick returned my midterm exam. What he did for me then changed my life.

I approached the exam like I had every test in those days: with minimum preparation and low expectations. When Mr. Nick returned the blue exam booklet, the only mark on it was the "B" he'd written on the cover. I knew I didn't deserve the grade; I also knew that a B felt pretty damn good. I never received less than a B from Mr. Nick. I even scored the occasional A. And I earned every one of them.

Life is filled with defining moments if we are lucky or observant enough to see them for what they are.

Finding effective mentors is one of the most important things we can do. Great mentors make positive differences in our lives. Sometimes, if we are lucky, great mentors find us.

Years later I asked Mr. Nick why he'd gone out on a limb and taken a risk on me. He responded, "I had a feeling you didn't really know what it felt like to succeed." It was a lesson I've never forgotten.

It is important to understand that Robert Nicolls did not make me successful. He did not change the environment or his teaching style or dumb down his expectations. He made himself my ally by recognizing that he and I were equally invested in a successful outcome. He was a mentor helping a student locate talents he might not otherwise have discovered. Mr. Nick took a risk he didn't have to when he opened the door to success for me. I responded by recognizing his gesture for what it was and walking through the door into a new reality.

Over the years I've reached out to many people for advice and council. I have had many mentors, all of whom were important to me at various stages in my careers. You possess the ability to achieve your goals. The quest becomes a lot easier when you share them with people who are invested in your success.

History is rich in examples of successful alliances. During World War II, for example, the United States, Great Britain, and the Soviet Union allied for a clearly defined goal: to win the war. Although victory was critical to every member of the alliance, being allies did not mean they agreed on every point. To the contrary they disagreed more times than they agreed.

Nor did it mean they always liked each other. What the alliance did mean was that on the one goal that mattered, the one that had brought them together as allies, they were determined to succeed. Where they disagreed they sought compromise and accommodation while setting aside personal distrust as best they could. To Winston Churchill, the British prime minister, ridding the world of Nazism was too important to let any other thing prevent the accomplishment of that goal. President Franklin Roosevelt of the United States and Soviet leader Josef Stalin agreed. By allying, learning to leverage each other's strengths, and focusing on an endgame of monumental importance, the alliance succeeded.

You might argue that World War II was far bigger and more significant than getting a job after college, but that would be missing the point. Imagine any activity involving more than one person where coordination, trust, and mutual reliance are critical to a successful outcome. Team sports, acting, or the school orchestra are all examples where successful outcomes depend on successful alliances.

The same is true with the alliance you have with your parents. You won't always agree; it's probably healthier that you don't. If everyone is agreeing on everything, you're probably missing something.

Learn to talk about your goals. Be open and honest about what you think. The ultimate goal is for you to land a meaningful job after graduation, but you will encounter hundreds of smaller goals along the way. Strategizing as allies paves the way for achieving them. Allies work with each other to develop mutually agreed upon strategies. The most important phrase here is "work with." This is a team effort, and your success depends on your insistence on being a contributing member of the team. Never pass up the opportunity to take control of your destiny, but don't feel as if you have to do it alone.

Successful alliances require jointly developed expectations, so each party clearly understands its role. Achieving goals as a team requires that every member recognize that all participants will have different strengths and weaknesses.

In team sports success depends entirely on each teammate's ability to leave ego on the sidelines. Doing what's right for the team is what wins championships. As the late Vince Lombardi, legendary coach of the Green Bay Packers said, "Individual commitment to a group effort—that is what makes a team work, a company work, a society work, a civilization work."

If you think you are too young to assume greater control over your destiny, think again.

The best time to begin is right away. Students raised in cultures that support and encourage exploration, self-reliance, and self-leadership, and in which the leash is longer, have far greater chances of identifying their passions and skills faster than those who aren't.

Mistakes will happen. You will screw up. We did; you will. An important aspect in preparing for the future is to unlearn the dangerous assumption that says mistakes and failures are unacceptable. As Einstein said, "Anyone who has never made a mistake has never tried anything new." You want to get out of your comfort zone and try new things. Above all embrace change.

The Bottom Line

- Life is not about coddling. Coddling is not how you grow; it is how you stay small. At this stage in your life you don't want or need it.
- Ask yourself two questions:
  - Am I ready to assume greater responsibility for my actions?
  - Am I comfortable with the consequences?
- Winning is not about showing up.
- Winning is about training, experiencing the sting of failure, and learning to bounce back.
- Any argument that you are too young to make a difference is spurious.
- What you ultimately do with your life is your business. You can be a doctor or a pole dancer, a derivatives trader, a dietitian, or a surfer dude. The decision to choose a career in finance, law, medicine, the military, or the church should depend on what you want to do with your life—no more and no less.
- Your parents might dream of the day you discover a genetic link between male pattern baldness and gerbils, but that does not have to be your dream. Nor does it have to be your life sentence.
- Students raised in cultures that support and encourage exploration, self-reliance, and self-leadership, and in which the leash is longer, have far better chances of identifying their passions and skills faster than those who aren't.
- Build a team of personal advisors.
- Talk about your goals.
- If you think you are too young to take control of your own destiny, think again.

CHAPTER 9
Seven Ways to Be an Ally

Parents are so used to being the boss that you might have to remind them what it takes to be your ally. Asking them to partner with you can be a difficult concept for them to grasp. Somehow it just doesn't sound particularly realistic; "Kids aren't partners, they're kids!"

Ask them to remember the best bosses they ever had. If they were fortune enough to have an effective leader as a boss, they never felt bossed.

Here's what you want to tell them:

1. Remember: This Is About Me

It is said that the future is about the young. Why then does it seem to the young that their futures are about the old?

Maybe you've had a problem similar to the one Jack, at the time a junior in high school, was having with his father. His father, who had inherited a family business from his own father, was putting pressure on Jack to follow the same path. Jack had no desire to go into the business but didn't know how to tell his father. Jack is very creative, an excellent writer and musician, and a conceptual thinker. The skills required to work in his father's company were not in line with his skills or interests.

The real issue was not Jack's suitability for a particular career; it was that his father was projecting his own wishes on Jack. According to Jack, his father ignored the fact that his interests did not involve working in the family business. It's not surprising that his father would want his son to follow in his footsteps. What father wouldn't? But that reflected his own dream, not Jack's.

You want your parents to bury the urge to tell you that they want you to take over the family business or go to law school or be a doctor or anything else for that matter. Cattle are herded into chutes according to size and shape. You don't want to be part of a herd. Explore your options and opportunities so you can decide on your own what you will do in the future.

It is very difficult to discover what you really want to do unless you are free to do so. Many parents, looking back on their own careers, admit they chose the paths they had thought were expected of them.

Encouraging you to pursue your passions can be transformative.

2. I Don't Need To Be Don't Micromanaged

Micromanaging is not teaching, leading, or, for that matter, effective management. Micromanagers communicate distrust, inhibit personal development, and retard progress. Parenting is the quintessential leadership position: you need a strong leader, not a micromanager.

Kelly was accepted to college and became animated as she talked about how much she looked forward to the next chapter in her life. I asked about her interests and if she knew what she wanted to study. "I'm really not sure what I want to do, and I'd like to take a lot of different courses. You know, explore stuff. But my mom is making me major in economics." When I asked her why, she said her mother, an economist, felt economics would provide a strong basis for any career she might pursue.

While Kelly might find she enjoys economics, heading to college with that major as a mandate as opposed to a possibility is nothing more than a crapshoot. There is no guarantee she will enjoy it, and in any event, by requiring that she concentrate on economics, her mother is depriving her of important opportunities for self-discovery.

You will excel at what you do if you are engaged in activities of your own choosing. Kelly dreamed of discovering her options. While a basic understanding of economics is important, left to her own devices she might find that her interests are in a different field altogether—or not. The point is that the decision should ultimately be hers.

Study for the sake of study is very different from pursuing a genuine interest—a reality that will make a big difference when you start interviewing for jobs. Employers look for passion and enthusiasm as well as a level of expertise. When you've been allowed to pursue your interests, you will communicate enthusiasm for, greater depth of understanding in, and commitment to your chosen field.

Art and Karen enthusiastically support their children's interests and see the college years as a Petrie dish for their futures. The couple owns a successful nursery and garden supply business, which they founded almost thirty years ago. They have four children and would have been thrilled if one of them had joined the business. But they always made it clear that whether or not they chose to do so was up to their children. So far each has chosen a different path.

"The nursery is there if they want it," says Art, "but it's their call entirely. Ultimately they have to do what is best for them, and that means doing what makes them happy. I'm just proud that they are all doing what they want."

The path that ultimately led their daughter to her career illustrates the power of discovery. Terry enrolled in a small liberal-arts college, planning to major in art history. By chance she discovered her passion and chose an entirely different major in the second semester of her freshman year. Terry was required to take a science course to fulfill part of the core curriculum requirement. She had a lot of science in high school and knew she didn't want to take any more than the bare minimum needed in order to graduate. What she hadn't considered was that college gave her the opportunity to take courses her high school had not offered.

In order to fulfill her requirement, Terry took a geology course called Natural Disasters. "The class was about earthquakes and volcanoes, stuff like that. All of a sudden, I remembered that when I was a kid I was fascinated by storms and earthquakes, so I decided to go for it."

Terry's chance encounter with this class was a transformative moment. She ended up majoring in geology with an emphasis in volcanology. She spent several weeks studying Montserrat Volcano in the Caribbean and a month in Alaska, where she studied the effects of seismic activity.

After graduating, Terry landed a job as an oil-field geologist working on drill sites in California and Alaska's North Slope. She later earned her masters degree in geology and continues to pursue her interest in volcanoes.

Terry credits her parents with creating an environment in which she was allowed to find her own passion. "My parents jokingly accused me of taking 'Rocks for Jocks' when I told them I was taking geology, but really they just wanted me to find something that was interesting to me," she said. "The only thing they ever said regarding what I took in college was that they preferred I go into a liberal-arts program and stay generic until I found something I really liked."

3. Please Introduce Me To The Possibilities

The "what do I do with my life?" process is stressful enough without parents' unwittingly adding to it. A friend tells a marvelous story about her daughter: "When Emily was about five, one of her relatives asked her what she would like to be when she grew up. Emily considered the question for a few seconds before responding: "What are the choices?"

That's just the point: what are the choices?

To Emily, who later majored in art history, the idea behind college was to learn as much as possible about interesting things. "I just don't want to put myself in a box," she said. "I mean, who at my age can really say they know what they want to do with the rest of their lives? I know I can't."

When you were young you probably jumped from one interest to another, maybe several times in the same day. One minute you want to be a fireman, the next a super model, and the next an astronaut. You never want to lose that. In a perfect world your parents will expose you to as many opportunities as possible and support you when you show interest. After all, how can you pursue your interests if you haven't explored the possibilities?

4. Absolutes Aren't Helpful

There are no absolutes in life—except, of course, that it will end. Saying things like, "if you don't get into the *right* school, you'll never get a decent job," and, "the only way you will get a decent job is if you major in business," is as unfair as it is untrue. Such comments, which are undoubtedly intended to encourage students, actually do far more harm than good.

There are five problems with absolutes.

First, absolutes close options, and options are what life is about. Second, by declaring something to be an absolute truth, we are in effect imposing our own wills. College is a place for students to find their way; it's the ultimate Petrie dish of life. Expressing an opinion and making clear that it is only an opinion is very different from imposing a will.

Third, to express an opinion as an absolute is to manage top down, and top-down management is rarely as effective as collaborative leadership. It is no more than micromanagement. Since employers are telling us they value employees who can work in teams, it stands to reason that learning to collaborate should start at home.

The fourth problem with absolutes is that they set the stage for failure. One can imagine the sense of failure that can result if parents say to their child that graduation from an Ivy League school is the best ticket to success. Suppose the child, for whatever reason, is not accepted into an Ivy League school. She has failed to meet expectations, has let her parents down, and by proxy views anything other than Ivy League as a step down in education.

The fifth problem with absolutes is that they are frequently not true.

- "Sensible and responsible women do not want to vote"— Grover Cleveland, 1905.
- "Heavier-than-air flying machines are impossible"—Lord Kelvin, president of the British Royal Society, 1895.
- "Everything that can be invented has been invented"—Charles H. Duell, US Patent Office, 1899.

Innovation begins when we question convention and discard absolutes. Without people who challenge absolutes the world might still be flat, and the Earth might be the center of the universe.

5. Give Me Guidelines: Please Don't Hover

Tell me what you want done then leave it to me to figure out how to do it.

Effective leaders see greater value in clearly defined guidelines than in the rigidity of rules, which offer little room for exploration or interpretation.

They know that nurturing an environment that places a premium on creativity and critical thinking is a time-honored way to identify talent.

Giving you the responsibility to make your own decisions within the framework of clearly defined guidelines communicates trust. It helps you gain confidence in your abilities. You will make mistakes. So what? Shit happens. Making mistakes, taking responsibility for them, and fixing them are important steps in your maturation process. In the corporate world, it's one way that leaders develop future leadership. If a boss is a micromanager, he may never know the real value of an employee.

In the same way, as you get older you should want increasing amounts of decision-making responsibility. If you are required to stay within a narrowly defined set of rules and your every movement is monitored, it will be very difficult for you to discover the limits of your capabilities.

"Helicopter parent," "bulldozer parenting," and "tiger mom" are all pejoratives associated with micro-managing, top-down decision making and second-guessing.

Far from promoting critical thinking or effective problem-solving skills, they often result in self-doubt and indecision.

Mark and René created an environment in which they encouraged their two sons to experiment—within limits. Like all parents they created guidelines for their sons, who, like all children, tested the limits. Guidelines are different from rules; they imply a certain amount of latitude.

"Visualize a straight line," said Steve, "running from where you are standing to the horizon. That line represents the track our parents gave us to run on. Some parents might see it as an absolute, but even though they never really said so, my parents saw it as a guide."

He continued, "Now imagine there are two parallel lines, one about ten yards on either side of the guideline, that represent the latitude my parents gave me. If I strayed too far on either side of the line, they'd reel me in, but they expected me to test the limits of their rules and my abilities."

René added, "We had rules, but they were more like expectations about the kind of behavior we thought was important. We wanted the boys, first and foremost, to be good people, to treat other people well, and to be unfailingly honest. We impressed on them from a very early age that all decisions, good or bad, have consequences. Kids need to make mistakes. If they don't how can they learn?"

6. Support Me: Don't Do It For Me

My father would have chewed off his own arm before complaining to a coach that I wasn't getting enough playing time. A problem with a coach was my problem to solve. While my father might have offered suggestions on how to approach the conversation, he never would have run interference for me; to do so would have robbed me of an important life lesson.

Today it is common for parents to complain to coaches about playing time. Parents call teachers, not to discuss how students might improve their writing skills so they might get better grades, but to complain that the grades they received weren't high enough. Remember the e-mail from the parent with the overscheduled child? "An eighty will look much better than a seventy-four, so you need to change my child's midterm grade." What kind of messages did this child receive when her parent stepped in to demand a grade she did not deserve? Parents complain to college professors, accompany children to job interviews, and even appeal to employers if bonuses or raises aren't high enough.

Some of the most egregious examples of parental interference colleagues shared with me include:

- A parent called and asked why the "prettiest girl" (her daughter, if you didn't guess) wasn't in the photo slides on the school website.

- A parent called and demanded that the yearbook be reprinted since her "most accomplished" daughter wasn't prominently placed on both pages of her team's spread.
- A parent admitted to writing his child's essays because high school was simply a "stopping point"—the child was a tennis prodigy, he said, and bound to play at Wimbledon.
- A child placed on junior varsity as a sophomore was promised to swing (play on both varsity and junior varsity as needed). His father actually yelled at the coach for making the wrong decision since he had already written "varsity" on all the child's college forms.
- A parent complained that homework assignments were not communicated even though the homework was posted on the class webpage, e-mailed to the parent, and discussed several times in class.

Your parents' time is better spent preparing you to handle difficult situations as they arise instead of trying to solve problems for you. You have to learn to self-advocate.

7. Empower Me

We all know how good it feels to be empowered.

Being empowered means we are capable, trusted, and valuable. But empowerment doesn't happen because we tell people they are empowered; they earn it one step at a time. By assigning meaningful tasks, not make-work; defining the requirements; observing without hovering;

accepting mistakes; correcting without doing; and giving constructive criticism and a lot of attaboys, we empower.

The message needs to be clear: "I can forgive mistakes as long as you try."

The old adage that information is power isn't trite. Being comfortable with one's skills and innate talents is empowering. Training—for a big game, to run a marathon, to deliver a keynote address, or to try a case—is also empowering. Knowing who we are and our strengths and weaknesses as well as having goals and a plan to achieve them build confidence.

More than any person that I've met, Robert Nicolls knew how important it is to empower young people. His philosophy was built on empowering young men to make decisions. Many of his former students and players credit him with much of the success they earned later in life.

As a coach Nicolls believed in giving his players the power to make decisions on the field during games. He felt strongly that his job was to give his players the tools and confidence to succeed, and then to push decision making to the lowest level possible. "My job as a coach was to develop young people and prepare them to succeed as adults. Winning was secondary to that."

As a leader his greatest contribution was giving his players the confidence to risk being wrong. He put us on a long leash and never criticized us for taking risks. Because of that we were never afraid of making mistakes. That's what empowerment is all about - removing the stress of being wrong.

Nicolls had eight rules that guided his approach to his players:

- Be willing to be wrong.
- Give them responsibility.
- Let them solve problems on their own.
- Set goals.

- Create road maps to achieve goals.
- Use constructive criticism.
- Trust them.
- Support them.

The environment in which you are raised will have an important impact on what you ultimately become.

There is a big difference between pushing you to succeed and creating an environment in which you want to succeed. Pushing, cajoling, and threatening are counterproductive. Empowerment and confidence go hand in hand as forces that drive success.

Jason, an attorney in Washington, DC, is emphatic that the environment his parents created drove his success. "I have dysgraphia, a disorder that affects my ability to write. Quite literally I have to draw each letter slowly and deliberately, a process that takes a long time. Fortunately it was discovered when I was young, so my parents were able to take steps to be sure it didn't affect my schooling."

When Jason applied to colleges, his first choice was to attend an Ivy League school, but he was not accepted. He was accepted to a small liberal-arts college where he majored in political science and graduated with honors. He was then accepted to an Ivy League law school, where he made the law review.

According to Jason, "I once told my father that it was the environment in which I was raised that nurtured my success. My parents never pushed me to be something I didn't want to be, never saw dysgraphia as an impediment to success, and always made me feel as if I were capable of doing whatever it was I set out to do. Whenever I needed help, they were there for me. While they frequently taught me how to do things, they rarely did them for me. I was taught that if I really wanted something badly enough, the responsibility to get it was mine. Learning I was capable was incredibly empowering and the most important lesson my parents taught me."

Allying is really about helping you find a purpose, supporting your mission, and helping you to achieve your goals. It just makes sense, not just for you, but everyone who benefits by what you accomplish when you are doing what really engages you.

The Bottom Line

- Respectfully communicate:
  - The future is about me
  - I don't need to be micromanaged
  - Introduce me to the possibilities
  - Absolutes aren't useful
  - Give guidelines but please don't hover
  - Support me but don't do it for me
  - Empower me
- Explore your options and opportunities so you can decide on your own what you will do in the future.
- When you're allowed to pursue your interests, you will communicate enthusiasm and a greater depth of understanding in, and commitment to, your chosen field.
- Ask yourself: What are my choices?
- Innovation begins when we question convention and discard absolutes.
- Nurturing an environment that places a premium on creativity and critical thinking is a time-honored way to identify talent.
- Be your own self-advocate.
- Empowerment is earned, one step at a time.
- The old adage that information is power is not trite.
- The environment in which you are raised will have an important impact on who and what you become.
- Allying is really about helping *you* find a purpose, supporting *your* mission, and helping *you* to achieve *your* goals.

CHAPTER 10
You Never Listen!

Have you ever tried to convince someone of something, a parent for example, only to feel like you're talking to a brick wall? Nothing you say seems to get through.

I am willing to bet that everyone reading this has said, "You're not listening to me," or even, "You never listen to me." After seven years as a history teacher observing the relationships between parents and students, I conclude that you have a point: parents do too much talking and far too little listening. So do you.

Listening, really hearing what the other person is saying, deflects a lot of misunderstanding.

If you listen, really listen, to what the other person is saying you will steer him to your point of view far more often than you will by talking.

Through the generations, the inability to communicate effectively has been the root of many vexing problems—some great, others small. Most would have been avoidable had each side just listened to what the other was saying.

One evening in the early 1960s, my family sat at our usual places around the dining room table. One of my brothers said something that to me seemed obvious. I said, "duh."

"What does that mean," my father wanted to know.

"Everyone knows that." It was an accurate, if unfortunate, answer.

"I don't give a damn what everyone knows. I want to know what it means!" The force of my father's hand hitting the table lifted the dinnerware.

"Everyone knows that." I mean, how much clearer could I be?

"What does it mean?" By now my father was apoplectic.

"Everyone knows that!"

And on it went. The evening did not end well.

My father wasn't listening. To be fair, neither was I. As misunderstanding led to conflict, neither of us was able to see the absurdity to the situation we'd created. The generational filter is dense. Like parents and kids down through history we weren't communicating effectively.

Face it, when discussions with your parents dissolve into "winner-take-all arguments," you are rarely the winner.

Listening is key to effective communication. It's not just hearing and understanding what is being said. Listening is done with our ears and our eyes. Body language speaks volumes. We can communicate much without exchanging words.

When you do talk, make your point quickly and succinctly then listen for and observe the reaction. Anticipate objections. If there are any, you will be prepared to deal with them.

The weight of the evidence, judging by how few people listen effectively, is that it is a skill not easily mastered. Because most of us are more interested in expressing our own opinions than hearing what someone else is saying we often miss important opportunities to agree.

Listening is a critical skill. It's essential to effective communicating, while at the same time, the most difficult of the communication skills to master. As Winston Churchill said, "Courage is what it takes to stand up and speak. Courage is also what it takes to sit down and listen."

Effective listening is a skill shared by all successful sales professionals and, as I will discuss later, an interview is the ultimate sales pitch. A key element in any sales strategy is to avoid talking your way out of a sale. If, for instance, you want your parents to let you do something, try listening carefully to the objections they are certain to have before allowing the conversation to turn into an argument. Objections might be subtle so listen carefully.

Listening is not about winning arguments. Listening is about avoiding arguments by engaging each other in a different way.

Partners in a common goal will rarely agree on every point, but by understanding each other's concerns you will be able to find common ground and move forward to reach common goals.

It's difficult to recall an important concept or invention, from medical breakthroughs to personal computers that didn't begin with observation. Listening is observing. Whatever you choose as a career, your value to an organization, as well as your personal success, will be in direct proportion to what you do with what you observe. This includes how successful you are when persuading others that your ideas have merit. What better place to learn than in your own home.

Life is not a zero sum game; there is usually merit in both sides of a conversation. But without listening to what the other side is saying, agreement is elusive.

We get so wrapped up in trying to prove our point that we miss what the other party is saying. Listen for the real objections. Listen for points of agreement, no matter how small. Learn to say: *If I understand you correctly....* Once you know what someone else is thinking – his or her real objections – it is possible to find a solution that will satisfy everyone.

It's human nature to want to advance your own ideas. But as Katherine Hepburn's character reminds us in The *African Queen*, nature is what we are put on this earth to rise above. Rise above the urge to speak and take the first step toward controlling the outcome of a conversation.

Remember, to your parents you are a child, their child, regardless of how old you are. In this era of hovering and over-protecting they are slow to let go. Your task is to change the paradigm. You want your parents to see that you are capable of making good decisions and comfortable living with the consequences. They need to visualize you as a competent adult, as the professional you are becoming.

Think of listening as part of a grand strategy, especially when you are trying to sell an idea. You always want to plan your pitch in advance, and anticipate any objections. You want to manage the process so that you increase the chances for success.

Develop a goal. Any conversation in which you are asking for something, or for someone's approval, should start with you communicating what it is that you want. Don't hedge. What is it you want to do and why? Why is it important to you and what are the benefits?

One of the essential rules for interviewing is to remember that the interview is not about you. The same is true when you are asking for anything, including permission. It's about getting the other party, your parent's maybe, to say yes. To make headway in a discussion regarding opposing views it is important to understand what motivates the other side.

Anticipate objections and have responses ready. This will enable you to stick to the facts rather than getting bogged down in disagreement. Try repeating the objection before you address it. *So if I understand correctly, you're concerned that...*

Listen For Your Opportunity. A conversation can turn on a comment. Remember that listening is done with the eyes as well as ears. Body language speaks volumes about a person's mood, disposition, or inclination. *Something seems to trouble you about this. What is it that I need to address?* By asking you will learn the major obstacles that need to be overcome. Is it trust or lack of experience? Whatever the objection, you might never know unless you ask.

Don't make it personal. Don't get drawn into an argument that you're not going to win.

Arguing only serves to reinforce the other side's position – especially if the argument is with your parents. *You're not old enough – mature enough – practiced enough to....* There are opportunities hidden in different opinions. Look for points upon which to agree instead of focusing on disagreements.

Compromise does not mean loss and is often better than an unqualified no. A negotiation where one side wins and the other loses is not a successful negotiation. Take what you get this time. After you've proven that you can be relied on to do what you say your going to do, reach higher.

The Bottom Line

- Listening is key to effective communication. It's a critical skill.
- Listening, really hearing what the other person is saying, deflects a lot of misunderstanding.
- Effective listening is a skill shared by the most successful sales professionals.
- When you present an idea, get to the point quickly and succinctly.
- Observe reactions - verbal as well as physical.
- Anticipate objections in advance.
- Plan your responses in advance.
- Listen for your opportunity.
- Don't get drawn into an argument you're not going to win.
- Compromise does not mean loss. It's often better than an unqualified no.

CHAPTER 11
Follow Your Dream

Pete was a senior in high school when he told me he planned to study business in college. I asked him why. "My father was in the investment business and did pretty well. It seems like a good way to make money."

I asked him what he would do if money weren't the issue? Pete didn't hesitate: "I'd be an oceanographer."

If that was the case then why major in business? "I figure I can make a lot of money then quit and do what I really want to do."

Don't do it Pete! Follow your dream. Very few people manage to make that happen.

Why not major in oceanography and minor in business. You might ultimately opt for business but at least you've given yourself an option. Remember, you never want to look back at your career and ask yourself *what if*.

Don't get me wrong; there is nothing wrong with majoring in business or economics. At the very least, regardless of what you choose as a major, you should take introductory courses in economics, accounting and finance. No matter what career you ultimately pursue, you will be well served if you have a basic understanding of each.

> ### The decision to make a lot of money so that you can eventually quit and do what you really want to do is rarely a good decision.

Your interests may change. If you pursue them until you find you find your niche, it is less likely that you will find yourself in a box from which there is no escape.

The idea that you can make a lot of money before walking away to pursue a passion might be laudable, but it rarely happens. Don't do it!

I interviewed a lot of people who were drifting - unsure of what they really wanted in a career. One morning when I was the manager of the PaineWebber office in Baltimore, I interviewed Matt. Matt was a recent graduate of the University of Maryland.

My mother had been speaking with friends who mentioned that their son was looking for a job. She had volunteered to have me speak with him. When she called the following morning, I agreed to do so and suggested she have Matt call my secretary and set up an interview.

Matt was bright and personable, but the interview went badly. He was not the problem, at least not directly. The problem was that he had no idea what he wanted out of life and, as a result, was struggling to explain why he wanted to be a stockbroker, the job for which he was interviewing. Despite the obvious disconnect, I liked him; what began as an interview morphed into a constructive conversation.

We were about five minutes into our conversation; my interest had begun to wane after about thirty seconds. While Matt was trying his best, it was clear he had no idea what he really wanted to do. I might have been new at the job, but I knew a canned presentation when I heard it. People with passion don't need scripts to be convincing.

"So, why are you really here?" I said, interrupting him in midsentence.

"What do you mean?"

"I mean, who put you up to this? You and I both know you don't want to be in the investment business."

Matt paused, trying to figure out how to respond. "My parents. They just want me to get a job, and they keep getting me interviews for business-type positions. You know, sales and stuff like that."

"What do you want to do?"

"Honestly? I have no idea.

"Do you have any interests or passions you might want to pursue?"

"I don't know. Not really."

"OK. Here's the deal. You don't want to do this, and I'm not going to hire you anyway. Relax. Let's talk about what makes sense for you right now."

His body language changed the moment I said it, and as he relaxed I saw him for who he was: an energetic, smart, conversant individual who, like many his age, was struggling with identifying his talents and how best to use them.

Matt leaned forward, smiling. "Great. What should I do? My parents are all over me to find something, and I have no idea where to start."

He was adrift. No one had asked him what he wanted to do with his life. Like me, he'd never given any thought to a range of options. He told me he'd been a good if not exceptional student with excellent social skills, so there seemed to be an expectation that he'd find a respectable sales position and join the millions of nine-to-fivers for whom working was a means to an end. It was not an expectation he'd ever questioned, nor had he ever considered the alternatives.

"I'd take some time to figure out what you really want to do," I responded.

"What do you suggest?" Matt asked.

To this day I'm not sure why I responded as I did, although at some level I must have been revealing a suppressed desire to follow the advice I was about to give.

Back then, when travel was easier and less expensive, it was possible to buy a one-year, round-the-world ticket from a major airline like Pan Am. A traveler paid $1,000 for a ticket that was good for a year and allowed him to fly east to west or west to east. Side trips north or south were permitted, but once you'd started you could not go backward. To me it was the perfect answer to Matt's dilemma.

"If I were you, I'd buy one of the Pan Am round-the-world tickets and have an adventure while you're trying to figure out what to do with your life. In the long run, spending a year making decisions and navigating different cultures will make you more attractive to an employer. It's hard to imagine that the experience won't open a window to your future. Face it, anyone you want to work for is going to be intrigued by what you've done."

Matt was transformed by the time he left my office. I wished him luck, and he thanked me profusely for giving him "the best advice I've ever gotten!"

The next day my mother called me again. "What in the hell did you tell that kid?" She demanded without bothering to say hello.

"Hi, Mom."

"What in the hell did you tell Matt? Did you really tell him to buy a ticket and spend a year flying around the world? What were you thinking? His parents are furious!" Needless to say, she never volunteered my services again.

I don't know what Matt ultimately did with his life, but I hope he didn't follow his parents' expectations and spend his life regretting that he hadn't done something else. I certainly don't regret giving him the advice or invoking his parent's anger. As Matt and I spoke, it occurred to me that I was giving advice I'd never received. It was a conversation I wish I'd sought and advice I wish I'd been given.

The more I thought about it, the more I liked the idea. The more recent graduates I interviewed, the more I realized that far too many were drifting through life without a clue as to what they wanted out of the experience. Few graduates with whom I spoke communicated well thought out senses of mission. Although some seemed clear in their ambitions, it was difficult for me to accept that they were, in their young twenties, ready to commit themselves to lives as stockbrokers.

My conversation with Matt was not the last time I suggested that someone consider taking a gap year before starting a career. A few months later, a seasoned broker in the office introduced me to Dave, also a recent graduate of the University of Maryland. As a favor to my broker, I interviewed Dave although I'd already made up my mind not to hire him. At the time my business plan committed me to recruiting established brokers from the competition. Recruiting was less expensive, added immediate revenue, and was far less labor intensive.

As it turned out, Dave had all the attributes of an outstanding broker: he was bright, energetic, conversant, motivated, and competitive. Despite all that, I decided not to hire him.

"I don't want to invest what it takes to train you," I explained, "only to have you decide later that you're looking for something else in life."

That was partly true. I had also determined that if he got a competitor to hire and train him, it would be a lot less expensive for me to recruit him in the future than to hire him myself.

"Look, Dave, I think you're an excellent candidate," I went on, "but I have to pass. You need to get some life experience, prove to yourself that this is what you really want to do, and then come back in a year or so, and I'll hire you.

"So, what should I do?"

I responded by giving him the same advice I'd given Matt. Dave said the idea was intriguing...and then took a job with a competitor. He passed the requisite tests to become a broker and built an impressive clientele.

Dave was an immediate success. A year later, when it was clear I'd made a mistake, I took him to lunch, ate the requisite amount of crow, and tried to recruit him. He was cordial as he essentially told me that he had given me the first opportunity to hire him, and I'd blown it. Yet as we lingered over lunch, I still wasn't convinced of his long-term commitment to the brokerage business.

A year later Paine Webber transferred me to New York to run the retail branch office in lower Manhattan, which was experiencing significant problems. After struggling for over a year to fix the problems and to stabilize and rebuild the office, I felt comfortable enough to take a much-needed two-week vacation in Mykonos, one of the Greek Islands. Near the end of the first week as I sat in Niko's Taverna nursing a pitcher of chilled Greek wine and enjoying the magnificent sunset, a voice behind me said, "Tim! What the hell are you doing here?"

It was Dave. He joined me for dinner. Over fresh calamari, Greek salad, and more wine than we needed, he told me he'd arrived in

Mykonos from Italy, where he'd been for two weeks. All in all he'd been in Europe for a month. I asked him how he could afford to be away from his clients for that long.

"I quit," he said.

"Why did you do that?" I asked. "The last I heard, you were a huge success."

"Yeah, I was doing well. And I really enjoyed what I was doing at Bache, but I could never get our conversation out of my mind."

"Which part?"

"The part where you told me to travel—to get some life experience."

Ah, sweet vindication!

Dave left Mykonos a few days later. He travelled for nine months to places like Israel; India; the Maldives; and Myanmar, or Burma as it was called then. By the time he got to Bangkok, he'd traveled enough. Not ready to return to the States, he forfeited his Pan Am ticket and went to Paris, where he landed a job with Kidder Peabody, selling securities to institutions in the Benelux countries. After three years as an expatriate, Dave decided it was time to return to the United States to continue his career in the investment business.

In short Dave's instincts were good. Pursuing a career in the investment business was right for him. In a sense my instincts were also correct. Like many new professionals, Dave got restless. Unlike most of us, who live with our restlessness, he decided to explore the reasons behind it. While too many of us toil at jobs that do not satisfy, Dave acted on his intuition. It wasn't that he was unhappy; like many young people, he was simply restless. He was unattached and had few responsibilities other than his job, so he decided that "what if?" was not a question he could leave unanswered.

In his commencement address at Roanoke College in 2010, author John Jacob Scherer said, "A mid-life crisis is when you get to the top rung of your ladder only to realize that you leaned it against the wrong wall."

Don't let that happen to you. I used to see people pouring out of their offices in lower Manhattan, joining thousands of others, clawing over each other to get a seat on the subway, headed home to escape another day. Many of them wore the thousand-yard stare; that dazed look that says, "How did I get trapped in this shit pool."

You don't have to live that way.

Explore your options: be curious, test your limits, try new things, travel and meet people who are different than you.

Try it all, but don't settle.

The Bottom Line

- The decision to make a lot of money so that you can eventually quit and do what you really want to do is rarely a good decision.
- The idea that you can make a lot of money before walking away to pursue a passion might be laudable, but it rarely happens.
- People with passions don't need scripts to be convincing.
- Sometimes a gap year after college is an excellent way to figure out what you really want in a career.
- "What if" is not a question you want to leave unanswered.
- Too many people toil at jobs that don't satisfy.
- Explore your options:
  - Be curious
  - Test new things
  - Travel
  - Meet people who are different than you

CHAPTER 12

A Career In Sales... No Way!

An embarrassing silence interrupted our conversation. I could almost hear the thought waves reverberating in the minds of the science majors: "You've gotta be kidding me! I didn't spend four years in college for this shit. Not me; I'm going to Med School!"

I'd just asked students at Muhlenberg College if anyone was considering a career in sales. They probably wondered if they'd walked into the wrong meeting.

Listen up science major. Whether you like it or not, you're in the sales business and will be everyday of your life if you want to be successful.

Brain surgeons psychologists, engineers, you name it, they are all in the sales business. They have to be and so do you.

I was in the sales business for my entire career, as a stockbroker, sales manager, and chairman of the sales division of a large mutual fund company. After becoming a teacher I discovered that the best teachers understood better than most how important sales is to the profession.

I once asked a successful sales professional how he did so well, year after year. "I always keep in mind," he told me, "people like doing business with friends." Knowing how to make a connection is the first step in gaining trust and building a friendship. Clearly, there's much more to sales than friendship, but if you remember that one thing - "people like doing business with friends" - the rest is easy.

A job interview is one of the most important sales pitches you will ever make. You are the product and you're selling yourself. Understanding the importance of developing a rapport is key to your success.

The first person I ever hired also happened to be one of the first people I ever interviewed. After I was appointed assistant manager of the PaineWebber office in Denver my boss handed me Elaine's résumé. Elaine had recently moved to Denver from her hometown in Connecticut. After reviewing the resume, I had all but decided she was a bad bet. I questioned why we would take the time to interview a woman who was new in town and who had no contacts or experience in business or sales.

Ignoring my reservations, he strongly suggested I talk to her: "I think you should find the time." I scheduled an interview—one of the first I ever conducted.

When we met I challenged Elaine: "I see you've spent the last five years as a teacher. What makes you think you can sell?"

Unfazed, Elaine looked at me as if I was a bit dim. "You've never been a teacher, have you?" Her answer put me off guard.

"What's your point?" I responded.

"Ever have a teacher that made you want to learn? Anyone can stand up in front of a class and dump a lot of useless information. Students learn if they like their teacher, right? I don't imagine the skills that made me a good teacher are much different than the ones I need to be a successful broker."

Although I doubt either one of us realized it at the time, with her answer Elaine accomplished two things. First, she illustrated how important it is to turn an interview into a dialogue. It was a classic sales method. Put the buyer at ease. As she engaged me in conversation, any reservations I had melted away.

Second, by answering my question with a question, Elaine took control of the interview. She couldn't have convinced me had she not first turned my interrogation into a friendly conversation.

Elaine's question turned a stilted by-the-book interview into a constructive conversation. That's the key to interview success. Many interviews feel like interrogations. Interrogations aren't friendly - conversations are.

Interviews don't have to feel that way. Listen for your opportunity; ask a probing question.

You can control the dynamics of your interview.

Excellent communication skills and the ability to work in teams are two attributes that employers look for. Allow your interviewer to imagine you as a member of the team. Give your interviewer reasons to consider your application. Make a connection.

Unfortunately too many interviews are driven by your resume, and let's be honest, if you're a recent graduate there isn't much on it. Your resume doesn't tell anyone who you are; it's a list of the few things you've done: mostly summer jobs and internships. When your interviewer says, "Tell me about yourself," don't make the mistake of parroting information she's already read. This is your chance to let her know who you are.

Express confidence, establish value, ask insightful questions and give answers that invite constructive dialogue. Asking about a company's vacation policy won't put you on the fast track to a career. Instead, try asking about an organization's position in its industry and what steps it is taking to gain market share in a competitive environment.

People like to talk about themselves. They also like talking about their organizations and what they do for the organization. Use this to your advantage. Show interest in the interviewer. Use open-ended questions as a prompt to encourage them to open up about themselves, their career paths, and their companies. Doing so can dramatically shift the tone and direction of your interview. It's how friendships are created, and people do business with friends.

Reflecting on my interview with Elaine and the many other interviews I conducted during my career, I realize that the most successful people I hired possessed similar qualities. They were passionate, enthusiastic, confident, and goal oriented. The most successful possessed critical attributes that reliably predicted their future success including:

1. **They were certain of the career they'd chosen:** The most successful were certain of their career path and able to explain why it was the right choice.
2. **Each was critically self-aware:** The most successful knew their strengths. They also recognized and were upfront about their weaknesses and how they'd learned to compensate for them.

3. **They were excellent communicators:** The most successful knew what they wanted in their careers and were able to explain what it was, why it was important to them, and how the jobs they were interviewing for reflected their real interests or passions. Verbal, written and listening skills were outstanding.

4. **Each articulated a sense of mission:** The most successful individuals I hired understood that to attain anything worthwhile, one has to see doing so as a mission. Those with personal missions found it easier to appreciate the importance of corporate missions.

5. **Each had written goals:** The most successful had life goals. They saw goals as essential blueprints for measuring progress. They understood that short- and intermediate-term goals serve as benchmarks leading to the successful completion of a mission.

6. **Each was prepared for their interview:** The most successful did their homework in advance. They researched the company, competition and industry. They researched the position they were interviewing for, and came prepared with questions.

7. **They were interview savvy:** The most successful were extremely savvy interviewers. Because they were good listeners, they were able to turn interrogations into conversations by asking relevant, open-ended questions.

8. **Each articulated how they could add value:** The most successful identified the needs of the company and illustrated how their skills and expertise would benefit it. They clearly understood that in hiring them, I was taking a risk and making an investment. They won me over by making me see their value.

9. **They were in character:** The most successful understood the importance of first-impressions. In the movie *Miss Congeniality*,

Michael Caine, playing beauty-pageant coach Victor Melling, offers exceptional advice to Sandra Bullock's Gracie Hart: *Wear the crown. Be the crown. You are the crown.* Taking the time to understand the look and language of a career is important.

10. **Each was unfailingly polite:** The most successful appreciated the importance of etiquette. We are a far more casual society than we once were. But manners are manners. They were on time for their interviews and never failed to send follow-up notes thanking me for my time.

This is not to suggest that the most successful fit a particular mold. To the contrary, each was an individual, with a unique personality and skill set. Some were extroverts while others were reserved. Some were damned difficult to work with. All were extremely good at what they did.

It's been thirty-five years since I hired Elaine, and she is still in the investment business, helping a substantial, high-net-worth clientele manage their assets. While she didn't have a background in finance or economics, she had excellent people skills and communicated her goals and ambitions clearly.

Looking back on the experience, I realize how many important lessons I learned from our interview: the résumé does not tell the whole story; skills are transferable; passion is a prerequisite; and if a candidate engaged me in conversation I'd better listen.

There is a reality you never want to forget: people do business with friends. As Lincoln said, "if you wish to win a man over to your ideas, you must first make him your friend." Elaine made a connection; after over thirty-five years we are still friends. Her ability to cultivate friend-ships earned her a job and helped her build and retain an impressive clientele.

Develop that skill science major -- it will serve you well.

The Bottom Line

- Whatever your profession, you're in the sales business, and will be every day of your career if you want to be successful.
- A job interview is one of the most important sales pitches you will ever make. You are the product and you are selling yourself. Understanding the importance of developing a rapport is key to your success.
- People like doing business with friends.
- Turn an interview into a dialogue.
- Interrogations aren't friendly - conversations are.
- You have the opportunity to control an interview.
- Employers value excellent communication skills.
- Express confidence, establish value, ask insightful questions and give answers that invite constructive dialogue.
- People like to talk about themselves. They also like talking about their organizations and what they do for the organization. Use this to your advantage.
- The most successful people I hired possessed ten critical attributes.
  - Certain of the career they'd chosen
  - Critically self-aware
  - Excellent communicators
  - Articulated a sense of mission
  - Had written goals
  - Prepared for their interview
  - Interview Savvy
  - Articulated how they would add value
  - Were in character
  - Unfailingly polite

CHAPTER 13
Resumes Are A Fool's Game

John Hunter, a senior career consultant with Lee Hecht Harrison, believes that networking accounts for eighty-percent of all hiring. Assuming he's correct -- I suspect he is -- why are so many college career counselors telling you to send your resumes or post your resume on Monster.com?

Most people I meet with are frustrated by the time they come to me for help. They've blanketed the market with resumes and have little to show for their efforts. They tell me they feel like losers.

If this is your experience I have two thoughts: 1) Mass mailing your resume *is* most often an exercise in futility and 2) You are *not* a loser. It's not your fault. You've probably never been taught how to network, or even how important networking is to finding a job.

If you want to land that killer job in the career you've dreamed of, save your postage and start networking.

Networking is a critical skill. Understanding why and knowing how will serve you well in the future.

Global connectivity and instant access to information has created a world increasingly driven by relationships. Connect: connect with your friends and their parents and your parent's friends, and your professors. Every successful person you've ever met understands the value of networking. They get it because it's how they became successful.

Mass-mailing resumes is a fool's game. Your résumé is important, but using it as a door opener is most often leads to frustration. You know you are perfect for a job that was recently posted on a corporate website. Unfortunately so are the multitudes of equally qualified applicants who are applying for the same job. Your resume, that one page outline of your life story, lands on the desk of someone unknown to you who will decide which of the faceless names will be offered interviews. The process is impersonal and inexact.

Most likely you've carefully crafted your résumé to get the attention of a screener. However, there are two problems with this approach. First, everyone else applying for the position has done the same thing. Second, even if you've crafted a genuinely kick-ass résumé, you have no idea who is going to review it. You have no idea what will appeal to him or her or what this person's mood will be on any given day. To make matters worse, it's not always a human deciding who gets an interview and who gets rejected. An increasing number of organizations create computer matrices to flag certain resumes.

Unless the stars are all aligned in your favor, and they rarely are, the likelihood that your resume will make it to the top of the pile is slim. Better to avoid the agony of mass mailing and network your way to an opportunity instead.

Resumes don't tell anyone who you are; they list what you've done. Networking builds relationships.

It's how you create opportunity in this increasingly relationship-driven world. Everyone you know, everyone they know and everyone you wish you knew is a potential resource, just as you are a resource for them.

The purpose of networking is to get in front of a senior decision maker so you can demonstrate your value in person. In other words you want to bypass the bureaucracy and get right to the top. In a competitive job market, you need to separate yourself from the pack.

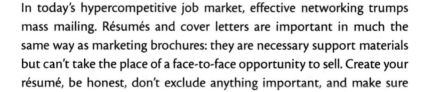

In today's hypercompetitive job market, effective networking trumps mass mailing. Résumés and cover letters are important in much the same way as marketing brochures: they are necessary support materials but can't take the place of a face-to-face opportunity to sell. Create your résumé, be honest, don't exclude anything important, and make sure spelling and grammar are correct. After that put it in a folder and don't produce it unless asked to do so.

You are part of the generation that made social networking a global phenomenon. How many "friends" do you have on Facebook? One thousand? Two? You have a wealth of information at your fingertips begging to be mined, sorted, and used to advance your ambitions.

Make social media work for you. If you are not already LinkedIn, it's time. When you link with a contact, you grow your network by being a part of her network. LinkedIn is not about who did what with whom last Friday night. It is a professional vehicle connecting you to other professionals. Each time you LinkIn with a new contact, you increase the probability that you are connected to a professional you can turn to for advice.

Effective networking gives you the opportunity to bypass the bureaucracy and start at the top.

Why endure several rounds of interviews before you finally get in front of the ultimate decision maker? In a competitive job market, who you know separates you from the pack faster and more efficiently than your resume.

Think of a networking meeting as a de facto interview. At this point you're merely asking for advice, however, any time you ask a contact for career advice you are being assessed. Are you a person he should hire? Is she comfortable recommending you to a friend or colleague?

When I met Emily, she'd recently graduated from college and was looking for a job in event planning. Emily grew up in a New Jersey community that feeds thousands of commuters into New York City. She has well over one thousand Facebook friends, many of whom have parents who live or work in New York.

Emily flooded the market with her resume for several months, but had nothing to show for her efforts. I asked if she knew any event planners or individuals whose organizations used event planners.

"No one," she responded. In fact, she did; she just didn't know where to look.

I asked Emily to think about her parents and her parent's friends, as well as her college friends and their parents. What about her Facebook friends? Someone she knew was probably with an organization that used event planners.

"Not really. At least no one I can think of."

Finally I asked Emily if any of her parent's friends or the parents of her own friends were senior executives with New York based corporations. Suddenly she understood.

"On yeah. And they're always holding meetings in some pretty cool places. I guess they probably use event planners - right?" Of course they do.

It's not just about whom you know. It's also about the people you know who are connected with someone you need to know. Networking is about mining contacts for leads and introductions.

⎯⎯ ⦇⦈ ⎯⎯

There is an art to asking for advice, which I will detail in the next chapter. For now consider this: looking for a job is competitive business. A lot of people are vying for the same job -- that job you know is perfect for you.

Give yourself an edge; never stop building your contact list. Make it a life-habit. Start now and never give up.

Not only is networking the most direct path to the career you want, it is an essential life skill. In a world that is increasingly driven by relationships, the ability to establish them for the benefit of everyone involved is a measurable asset. Networking is not just accumulating names. It is the process of building relationships that are mutually beneficial.

Networking is target marketing in the truest sense.

It is not simply having a lot of names: that is part of the process, but names without purpose are just names. Networking is about knowing how to use the names you have, and that means organizing them by industry, job title, and interests—any way that best serves your needs.

When you network you create opportunity. In this increasingly relationship-driven world, the ability to do so is a coveted skill. Friends, your parents, friends of parents, parents of friends and friends of friends are all potential resources just as you are a potential resource for them. As you study the names on your list of contacts, several will stand out as individuals you can turn to for advice. They are the ones most likely to hold the keys to the job you want.

The Bottom Line

- Mass-mailing resumes is a fools game.
- Your resume, that one page outline of your life story, lands on the desk of someone unknown to you who will decide which of the faceless names will be offered interviews. The process is impersonal and inexact.
- Resumes only list what you've done.
- Every successful person understands the value of networking.
- Networking is the most direct path to the career you want.
- Effective networking bypasses the bureaucracy.
- Networking is target marketing in the truest sense.
- The purpose of networking is to create opportunity by getting in front of decision makers.
- Make social media work for you.
- Think of a networking appointment as an interview with a different name.
- Effective networking creates opportunities.

CHAPTER 14
Networking Made Simple

There are many ways to network. After you land a job, and as you become successful in your chosen career, you will find creative ways to build relationships. For now, in order to achieve your immediate goal, follow seven important networking steps.

1. Build a Contact List

The first step in effective networking is to gather contacts. Get in the habit early of connecting with everyone with whom you come into contact. Maybe you already do this through Facebook. Now you need to connect with people who can make positive differences in your life. Develop the habit in high school and never stop.

By the time you are a junior in college and beginning the job search in earnest, you should have several hundred contacts.

Without contacts networking is impossible; as trite as it sounds, who you know really does trump what you know as long as you know how to mine your contact list.

At this point you might not realize how many valuable contacts you already have. When I first asked Emily who might be able to help her, she told me she didn't know of anyone with connections to the event planning business. As I probed she realized she didn't know any event planners, but she knew plenty of corporate executives.

"Do you suppose any of those people sponsor events?" I asked and then suggested she talk to them about whom they knew and whether they'd be willing to make introductions. I further suggested she research their organizations to find out if they had their own event planning departments.

Emmy needed to determine whom, of her one thousand Facebook friends, might be able to help. She narrowed the list to approximately fifty real friends and messaged them about her ambitions; she also asked if any of their parents were involved with event planning. As it turned out, several were.

By the time we finished exploring her contacts, Emily found she had many with ties to the event planning business.

2. Narrow Your Focus

Networking to achieve a specific goal is target marketing. For your purposes the concept is quite simple, requiring that you identify two things. First, you need to be clear what your goal is. Define as narrowly as possible the career and job you are looking for. Write them down, and don't waste time and energy pursuing jobs that don't meet the strict parameters of your goal.

Second, do your research. Create a list of people who have the highest probability of helping you attain your goals. Emily began her research by asking her parents about their friends, and her friends about their parents. She approached her college alumni office with a clear picture of the alumni she hoped to meet.

Networking is about focus.

Be as patient as a sniper: pick a target—in this case organizations and individuals that best represent the career you want. Indiscriminately submitting résumés, the shotgun approach to finding a career, is a temporary placebo. While activity might make you feel productive, it rarely produces results, leads to frustration, and causes paralysis.

3. Schedule the Appointment

If you are not comfortable calling people you barely know and asking them for favors you are not alone. The very thought of picking up the phone and making a cold call or even a warm call is daunting. The phone gets heavy; your palms sweat, and your heart beats just a little faster. Don't let that get in your way. It happens to everyone, even experienced telephone sales professionals. If you've never done it before, you have to put your goals before your fears.

One way to reduce anxiety is to have a mutual friend set the stage before you make your call. If, for instance, your dream is to pursue a career in oceanography, and your roommate's mother happens to be a director at Woods Hole Oceanographic Institution, ask your roommate to make a call on your behalf. She can ask her mother if she has time to speak and, assuming she does, tell her to expect your call. In this way introductions have been made, and you don't have to explain who you are and why you are calling. This should make the process much less intimidating.

> Aim as high up the corporate ladder as you can. A meeting with a senior vice president or even the CEO is far more likely to have a positive result than a meeting with someone with less authority.

Scheduling an appointment should always be done in person or by phone. Even in today's e-mail/texting culture, a phone call is the appropriate way to approach individuals with whom you want to network. They are often at least a generation ahead of you and use the phone for speaking, not texting. In fact both text and e-mail are impersonal methods of communication. Networking is personal, so unless e-mail is the only way to connect, pick up the phone.

Your initial call should be brief, to the point, and professional. This is an example of a possible approach:

Hello Mr./Ms. _____. As you may know [or as _____ may have told you], I will be graduating from _____ in May. I have given a lot of thought to what I want to do next and, I want a career in _____. Although you're busy, I'm hoping you have thirty minutes when we can meet. At this point I'm not asking for a job. I'm doing my research and know I will benefit from your advice and guidance on how best to proceed.

This is a particularly effective approach because it says a lot about you and appeals to a successful individual's sense of importance. You get to the point by saying exactly why you are calling. You communicate that you have a vision and goals. You acknowledge his or her importance by communicating that you know his or her time is valuable and asking for a short meeting. Finally, you have a clearly stated agenda: you want advice and guidance. Guidance is important. By saying "guidance" you are preparing to ask for referrals, which are key as networking is about meeting new people.

Asking for advice and guidance also appeals to ego and altruism. Do not underestimate the power of asking a successful person for advice. First, he or she will be flattered you asked. Second, many successful individuals see mentoring as an essential responsibility. After all, the boss is always on the lookout for talent. Successful hiring is essential to an organization's future. It means new energy, fresh perspectives, and an impressive pool of talent from which strong leaders will emerge.

In case you still feel uncomfortable making the call, remember: successful people became successful by doing the same thing.

4. Set the Stage

Once you have scheduled a meeting, you need to prepare for the event. Everything about you—what you say, how you dress, how much you know, the questions you ask, literally everything—communicates your value. Remember, a face-to-face networking meeting is an interview by another name. The person with whom you are speaking is not going to take you seriously, refer you to potential employers, or hire you if you are not prepared.

Your meeting can't ever look like a fishing expedition. Don't waste a busy person's valuable time when he or she is doing you a favor.

Remember: you have asked for thirty minutes, and you need to be prepared to end the meeting on time. If the individual with whom you are meeting chooses to extend the conversation, it is his or her option, not yours. This means you need to prepare for your meeting in advance, so you'll use the time as productively as possible.

To prepare:

A. Research Your Contact

Knowledge is empowering. It levels the playing field, allowing you to discuss your career ambitions with confidence. Know as much as possible about the person with whom you are meeting. Successful sales professionals know that closing a sale means developing a relationship; the more you know about your contact, the easier it is to create a relationship. Be sure to Google the individual before your meeting. At the very least, you will want to know the following:

- What is your connection to the individual?
- What is your contact's background?
- What does he or she do?
- What about your contact is noteworthy or newsworthy?

B. Research The Industry

You have scheduled a meeting to discuss your career ambitions; you need to know as much as possible about the field in which you are interested. Unless you want your contact to question your commitment, you should be able to demonstrate an impressive depth of knowledge. Once again the more you know, the more your confidence will be on display. You should be able to discuss the field in which you are interested:

- What is its purpose?
- To whom is it important?
- What is the size?
- Who are the major players?
- Is there recent press?

You have a plethora of resources at your disposal. Use the Internet, look for news sources, and ask your professors.

5. Critical First Impressions

As I've said a networking meeting is essentially an interview with another name. The contact you are meeting is gauging how well you will present yourself to people he or she might contact on your behalf. Always:

- Do reconnaissance in advance to know where you are going. Don't rely on GPS; it won't tell you if there are traffic issues or detours.
- Be on time for your meeting. Better yet be fifteen minutes early, so you'll have time to decompress, compose yourself, and freshen up.
- Dress the part. If you are interviewing for a Wall Street analyst position, don't go to your meeting in jeans and a belly shirt. Conversely if you are looking for a construction job, don't show up in a Paul Stuart suit.

- Don't wing it. Have an agenda.
- Anticipate the questions you might be asked.
- Prepare your own questions in advance.

6. Prepare Questions in Advance

Remember: you scheduled your meeting because you need advice and guidance, so that's what you'll want to ask your contact for. While you are making it clear that you are looking for a job, you do not want to ask your contact for one. Doing so changes the tone of your conversation by putting him or her on the defensive.

By asking questions you maintain an element of control over the direction of your conversation.

By mixing closed-end and open-ended questions, you engage in a conversation that stays focused while giving your contact the opportunity to be as expansive as he or she wants to be. People like to be given opportunities to talk about themselves and what they do for a living. Allowing them to do so is a fast way to build a relationship. Listen carefully to what is being said as you might find unanticipated opportunities to promote yourself.

Don't spend your meeting searching for questions; plan them in advance. Remember that opened-ended questions require expansive answers, which might lead to questions you hadn't considered. Listen carefully to your contact's answers, and look for opportunities.

Your questions might include:

- How did you decide this was the career for you, and how did you approach the process of finding a position?
- How do you feel about the business now?
- What specific advice do you have for someone trying to break into the business?
- Which firms do you think are the industry leaders?
- Are there specific individuals with whom I should meet?
- Would you be willing to make introductions for me?

7. Don't Leave Empty Handed

Remember, you requested your meeting because you need advice and guidance. Every piece of intelligence you accumulate will make you better prepared for future networking conversations and eventual interviews. In a sense you are going to school when meeting with your contact. Although a networking opportunity is not an interview, it is great practice for the real thing.

In a perfect world, you will leave your networking meeting with a job offer. It's possible, but don't be disappointed when you're not given an offer. Keep at it, and networking meetings will become interviews sooner than you expect.

Like any good sales professional, you want to ask for referrals. You need to know where your opportunities are, what organizations are hiring, and whom you should contact. In a sense networking is a numbers game—the more people you speak with and the more networking opportunities you find, the closer you are to landing a job. For example, suppose you schedule three networking meetings, and each contact agrees to introduce you to three individuals. Remember: networking is a full time job. The more you do it, the closer you are to a job offer.

8. Always Follow Up

As soon as possible after your meeting, send a thank you note. If your contact introduces you to other people in the organization, try to get their cards and send them follow-up notes. E-mail is fine, but nothing beats a thank you on personal stationery. Even better, send an immediate e-mail and follow up with a handwritten note as soon as you get home.

A note doesn't have to be long. Simply thank your contact for his or her time, be certain to say how much you value his or her advice, and ask for the opportunity to stay connected in the future. It is a very good idea to stay in the loop as your networking progresses. For instance, if he or she makes an introduction for you, be sure to let him or her know the results of the meeting.

It's one thing to make a connection, and another thing to cultivate and maintain connections. Networking is about building mutually beneficial relationships. Learn how to network early; your future success will depend on it.

The Bottom Line

- Collect names. Everyone knows someone with whom who might want to network.
- You already have more promising contacts than you think you have:
  - Parents
  - Friends of Parents
  - Friends
  - Friend's Parents
  - Professors
- Define as narrowly as possible the career and job you are looking for.
- Create a list of individuals that can best help you.
- Don't use a shotgun approach to networking. Be a sniper: pick targets that can help you advance your career ambitions.
- Aim as high up the corporate ladder as possible.
- Make your initial contact brief and to the point.
- Be prepared for your meeting.
  - Research your contact
  - Research the industry.
- Have questions. Questions do two things:
  - Indicate interest and knowledge.
  - Help you control the direction of your conversation.
- First impressions are critical.
- Ask for referrals
- Never forget a thank you note.
- Keep your contact in the loop as your search progresses.

CHAPTER 15
The Art Of The Interview

Sean has a B.A. in economics with minors in computer science and applied statistics. When we met he told me his goal was to find a position as an entry-level economist in New York. After a few years of practical experience he planned to get a graduate degree in economics, or maybe an MBA.

Sean's goals were ambitious to say the least. But as I listened, I tried to imagine Sean in a career defined by research, analytics, and green eyeshades. I couldn't.

Sean is extremely creative, outgoing, and communicative, all of which suggests that he might be better suited for a different career, one that combined his interests in business and technology with analytics and consulting. I kept my reservations to myself.

Sean's excellent networking skills resulted in interviews with several investment banks, but he never made it to the second round. Sean called me after a telephone interview for a position as an entry-level analyst. He knew he'd done poorly, and was angry and discouraged. I asked what he thought had gone wrong.

"It was the same as last time." His previous telephone interview had been for a similar position with an investment bank. "As soon as they asked me why I wanted to be an analyst, I froze. My heart started racing, and I was practically hyperventilating. It was a disaster."

I asked Sean why he thought he reacted so viscerally every time he was asked that question.

"I just don't know how to answer the question."

Maybe, I suggested, he had trouble answering the question because on some level he knew the job wasn't what he really wanted.

"I majored in economics. What else am I supposed to do?"

"How about something you really enjoy?" I responded.

Sean frequently talked about technology and technology startups. When he talked about friends who were in the business he seemed far more enthusiastic than when we talked about investment banking. Maybe you've been chasing the wrong career.

"I don't know. I've always thought I'd be an economist. I mean, don't I have too much invested to change directions now?"

"Sean," I told him, "your major doesn't have to be a life sentence."

Sean was twenty-two years old. Unless he hit the Powerball jackpot he'd probably be working for a long time. There is no rule requiring him to pursue a career as an analyst if he couldn't answer the question: *Why do you want to be an analyst?* I urged him to think about hobbies, classes or ideas that really interested him.

The next time we met Sean was energized, enthusiastic, and ready to move in a different direction. He decided to leverage his analytic background to land a career in consultative sales. Sean's revised goal was to find a position with a start-up technology company.

As it turned out, the shift in focus was just what Sean needed. The transformation was immediate: so was a job! Sean had several interviews and immediately received three excellent offers. Ultimately he accepted a position as a customer success analyst with a small, dynamic company specializing in search engine optimization.

It has been two years since he started his career and Sean is doing extremely well. Most important, he thoroughly enjoys his job.

⎯⎯ ✻ ⎯⎯

The problem leading to Sean's frustration is not unique. Many interviews fail because a square peg is being squeezed into a round hole. Self-confidence stands out in an interview.

It's not by accident that the most self-confident people I know are also the most self-aware.

They know themselves, what they like and dislike, and where they excel as well as their weaknesses and how to compensate for them. They know what they want out of life and have plans to achieve their goals. Knowledge is power; ignorance is not bliss.

There are two major mistakes interviewees make that prevent them from getting or, worse, keeping jobs. The first is trying to sell themselves as something they're not. They might fool potential employers into believing they have skills and interests they don't really have, but sooner or later they will be discovered. The second is not knowing or being able to communicate who they are and what they want in a career.

The important thing to remember is that you never want to fake it. There is a downside to pretending to be, or wanting to be, something you're not. You set yourself up for failure. You don't want a career to be your albatross. If you're not comfortable interviewing for a job maybe that little voice inside is telling you it's not the right job for you.

There are some exercises that will help you with your career decision. Call it foreplay—setting the stage to find the career that is right for you. The purpose of the exercise is to help you be as certain as possible that your skills and interests best support the careers you've chosen.

Start by answering seven questions honestly and completely:

1. Have you decided on a career? What is it?
2. If you have decided, how do you know it is right for you?
3. Did you make the decision yourself?
4. Do you have any hobbies, interests, or passions? What are they?
5. If your career choice and passions differ, does that suggest a conflict?
6. If you don't know what you want in a career, why not? What might be of interest and why?
7. Now that you've answered the previous questions, are you still certain the career you've chosen is right for you?

At some level everyone has a sense of his or her innate strengths and weaknesses. Knowing them and being able to communicate them to a prospective employer are two different things. It never fails to amaze me how many people have to search for answers when I asked them about strengths and weaknesses.

Self-awareness is empowering.

Employers are keenly interested in how potential employees approach problems, handle stress, and adapt to change. An honest appraisal in advance provides the confidence needed to perform well in an interview.

Next, answer the following three questions:

1. I am _____. (This should include your strengths as well as likes and dislikes.)
2. I am not _____. (This should include your weaknesses.)
3. Others see me as _____.

Create personal vision and mission statements. A dream is a vision of what might be and a mission is what you embark on when you set out to achieve your dream.

Great organizations have definable cultures that make them unique and set them apart from the competition. The culture is frequently reflected in the corporate vision. A personal vision is empowering; it says a great deal about who you are. The mission statement will help you stay focused.

Finally, develop goals. Goals give clarity to missions by dividing big challenges into manageable tasks. Many people see goals as burdens for the same reason successful people see them as essential to success. Goals focus, motivate, and guide; they keep a person honest and on track. Goals are a report card without which there is no way of grading progress. Break your goals into long-term goals, intermediate goals, and short-term goals. Be sure to note any roadblocks you might encounter.

In order to avoid frustration, try a simple exercise before pursuing your own career. Take a blank sheet of paper and draw a line down the middle. On the left, list those things you really enjoy doing, including activities you are passionate about. On the right, write down the career you plan to pursue.

Ask yourself this question: Does my current vision of a career reflect my interests and talents?

If the answer is no, rethink your career.

The Bottom Line

- Self-confident people are self-aware people.
- Self-confidence stands out in an interview.
- Don't pursue a career unless you are certain it is right for you.
- Don't fake it. Many interviews fail because a square peg is being squeezed into a round hole.
- Avoid the two major interview mistakes:
  - Trying to sell yourself as something your not.
  - Being unable to communicate who you are and what you want in a career.
- Make an honest appraisal by answering all the questions raised in this chapter.
- Create personal vision and mission statements.
- Goals give clarity to missions by dividing big challenges into manageable tasks.
- Ask yourself: Does my current vision of a career reflect my interests and talents? If not, rethink your career.

CHAPTER 16
You're Not a Commodity

Tyler was discouraged. A recent graduate whose goal was to land a position in technology sales, he'd had only a few interviews, but there were no job offers or even invitations to a second round of interviews. I had no doubts about Tyler's potential in technology sales. He is a facile conversationalist and a very good listener; he is a social, outgoing individual with well-developed networking skills. Tyler is multidimensional, well travelled, and a former college athlete who is artistic, creative, and innovative. Despite all of his many positive attributes, however, it was clear that something about his interview style wasn't working.

Tyler asked me to meet him for coffee so we could discuss his interviews, the most recent of which had taken place earlier in the week. At the end of the interview, he'd been told that he would be contacted the following morning if they wanted him to return for further talks. He had not received a call. Tyler's disappointment was obvious; he was beginning to doubt his decision and himself.

"Maybe I should think about doing something else," he said. "I feel like I'm being told I'm not made for technology sales."

"Maybe," I responded even though I was convinced it was the perfect career for Tyler. "But before you do, tell me about the interviews.

Let's see if we can figure out why you're not getting to the second round." I asked him to walk me through each of his interviews: with whom he spoke, what questions they asked, and how he answered them. It wasn't long before I'd heard enough.

"Frankly Tyler," I said, "If I were interviewing you, I wouldn't hire you either."

"What?" His frustration bordered on anger. "Why not? I did everything you told me to do. I did my research, arrived early, dressed the part, and asked questions. What am I missing?"

Tyler was right to a point. He had been well prepared for his interviews. His problem was that he was not saying or doing anything that made him stand out from the other individuals who were interviewing for the same jobs. He was not revealing himself beyond what he had included in his résumé. He was not using his interviews to communicate value to potential employers.

There are so many well-qualified recent graduates interviewing for jobs, all possessing similar skills and attributes, that hiring managers might be forgiven for feeling as if the candidates resemble commodities on the shelf at Home Depot.

No one wants to be thought of as a commodity, but without any distinguishing attributes that is precisely how an individual who interviews scores of people every day might see you.

If Tyler wanted to win an interview, he had to stand out. His value had to resonate; it was just that simple. People in the market for talent aren't grabbing products off the shelf. They are discerning shoppers in a buyer's market.

Because Tyler wasn't accentuating his assets, there was nothing to suggest he was any different from most of the individuals vying for the same job. His approach to interviews was to answer questions as they were asked. His passivity made it impossible for his interviewers to separate him from the competition. He hadn't used his innate sales skills to communicate the reasons why he was an investment with great potential. Since he didn't, Tyler allowed himself to become a commodity.

An interview is the ultimate sales pitch. When you interview for a job, you are selling a product, and the product is you. You need to know who should hire you, why, and how they will benefit by adding you to their team.

Salesmanship is an essential life skill. It is not coincidental that great leaders in virtually every field possess the uncanny ability to draw followers to their causes. They sell themselves, their visions, and their ideas; they create value, thus giving us reasons to follow their leads.

It is difficult to imagine a profession wherein sales skills are not essential to success. Great teachers sell something every time they stand in front of a class. Enthusiasm, expertise, and the ability to make lessons relevant are all important sales techniques. Lawyers, doctors, consultants, investment bankers, leaders in any profession all sell. We sell any time we try to convince someone to buy an idea or product. Whether one is pitching an investment idea or interviewing for a job, the skills that are needed to get to a yes are the same. Irrespective of one's job description, the ability to sell is crucial to success in one's career.

The essence of an interview is the ability to convince a potential employer that you represent value to the organization.

The ability to communicate value to an organization can mean the difference between success and failure. It's a skill you must learn.

Eric Melniczek, director of the career center at High Point University, believes one's ability to separate oneself from the crowd is an essential skill. According to Melniczek, "Branding allows you to successfully use what makes you unique and valuable as a job seeker. It lets you differentiate yourself from your peers, who are your competition, so you will stand out to hiring managers." Melniczek explains to students that while their uniqueness sets them apart, their abilities to demonstrate how that uniqueness can bring value to an organization will result in job offers.

Melniczek counsels HPU students that preparing for a job search means creating a brand, which requires intimate self-knowledge. It means learning the nuances of networking and interviewing and the critical importance of knowing the audience to whom you are selling. He is not teaching abstract skills. As a former executive recruiter, Melniczek has a wealth of hands-on experience. His background uniquely qualifies him for counseling students on how best to compete in today's job market.

Employers aren't impulse buyers. They have needs they must find the right individuals to satisfy. Now more than ever, employers can afford to be selective. It's a buyer's market, and the American workforce is not the only place to find talent. As recently as thirty years ago, a college senior was competing with his fellow students for jobs. Today competition is global. That is why it is so important that you acquire the essential elements of great interviewers.

Never assume that luck has anything to do with a job offer.

Success requires that you prepare carefully and develop a strategy to convince an employer of your value to an organization.

This means researching the company, knowing what the position entails, being confident of your ability to do the job, and knowing how to communicate your value to the organization.

Tyler and I decided to review basic sales skills and how they apply to an interview. Before doing that, however, we revisited our previous discussions about networking. Remember, a networking conversation is a de facto interview. The rules of preparation and engagement that apply to networking are the same that are used in an interview.

We then discussed how Tyler could incorporate basic sales techniques in his interviews. We started by talking about the research he must do before scheduling a sales call. Every prospect is unique, so it is reasonable to assume the needs of each are different. Questions to consider include: Who is the prospect? What does the prospect do? Does the prospect have a need for what you are selling, and if so why? You don't want to waste your valuable time, much less that of a potential employer, by interviewing for a position for which you are unsuited.

Next we talked about when and how to introduce features and benefits. A product has features that can be used to distinguish it from similar products. But discerning buyers don't buy features; they buy benefits.

That is, buyers have to see how the features are going to make positive differences in their lives.

Tyler was interviewing for a sales position, so it was important he demonstrate that he was already sales savvy. Doing so would send the message that he could generate revenues faster than other candidates.

Sales professionals anticipate objections in advance. If you've thoroughly researched the company and job requirements to be certain your career ambitions and skills are in line with what the position requires, there might not be any objections. But don't assume anything. Do your best to anticipate questions or objections.

Finally we discussed what questions to ask and when to ask them. Questions are powerful sales tools, and successful sales professionals are skilled at knowing when and what kind of questions to ask. It is important to ask the right kind of questions. Asking about benefits and vacation time in a first interview does not send the message that you are serious about a career.

Prepare open-ended questions in advance—well-formed questions that will demonstrate both interest and knowledge. Open-ended questions give an interviewer the opportunity to expand, which in turn can lead to follow-up questions and a conversation.

Questions have myriad purposes. At a minimum they:

1. Indicate interest.
2. Lead to dialogue.
3. Help establish a relationship.
4. Lead to unexpected answers and opportunities.
5. Allow you to gauge the interest of a prospect.

After revisiting how networking and basic sales skills apply to interviews, Tyler learned he could make himself truly stand out by exercising control over important aspects of an interview.

There are ways to control the tone and direction of an interview.

Start by relaxing. Be yourself. You don't yet have the job, so you have nothing to lose. Interviews can be intimidating, but with proper preparation they don't have to be.

We all perform best when we are in our comfort zone. Anticipate; try scripting your interview in advance. How the script evolves depends in part on the type of job for which you are interviewing. It also depends on your ability to turn an interview into a conversation between parties who possess common interests.

Understand and embrace four critical concepts:

1. The Interview Is Never About You

If you are interviewing for an entry-level position, your needs were established before you got to the interview. In that respect there is little to differentiate you from the many others who are vying for the same job.

Always remember you are at an interview because a company has needs, and those needs are greater than yours.

When you interview it is important that you be in character. Not only do you want to dress the part and speak the language of the career you want, but if you adopt the company's mission, vision, and culture as your own, your perceived value will be immediately apparent. Many companies publish this information on their websites. In the event that a company doesn't, do some digging, and speak to employees or customers. Find out as much as you can about not only the position but also what the company is about.

The company's mission statement will give you a great deal of information. Mission statements are inspiring words intended to communicate an organization's purpose and primary objectives. They help unify all employees in a common effort. Missions give employees a purpose or reason to come to work every day that transcends the narrow scope of their individual job descriptions.

An often-told story about President John F. Kennedy's visit to NASA in Houston, Texas, in 1961 illustrates the importance of having a mission. As the president toured NASA's headquarters, he stopped to ask employees what they did. One told him he was an engineer; another assembled parts of the launch platform, and so on. As he was leaving, Kennedy stopped to speak with a janitor who was mopping the floor.

"What do you do here?" asked the president as he shook the man's hand.

The janitor proudly replied, "Mr. President, I'm helping put a man on the moon!"

Does the company have a vision statement? Vision statements are similar to mission statements but add depth to them. Vision statements define an organization's values or guiding beliefs. That is, while an organization has a mission, there is a motivating purpose behind it -- something greater than profit, employee retention, and customer satisfaction.

Finally, some companies publish their guiding principles. Sometimes called "core values," these are statements that define what an organization strives to be every day of its existence. They serve to remind everyone that there is a set of values that dictates behavior and performance.

If you were a hiring manager, what would you look for in a candidate?

Naturally you would look for specific skill sets, but a lot of candidates have the skills you need. Odds are you will be drawn to candidates you can visualize as colleagues. Try putting yourself in the interviewer's shoes. Doing so will give clarity to your mission.

2. You Must Establish Value

You are not being hired as a part-time employee for as long as it takes to complete a specific task then being sent back to a temp agency. You are interviewing for a career, one with training and opportunities for increasing amounts of responsibility and promotions. As far as the hiring organization is concerned, you possess many of the elements of unrefined raw material. It will take time to train you, and time is money.

The organization is making an investment, but for the foreseeable future you are slotted in the P&L as an expense. At the earliest stages of your career, your value to the organization is measured by how quickly you become an asset. The organization is making an investment in you. It is interested in making a significant return on it quickly. Your task in an interview is to give the perception that you represent an investment with immediate returns.

Make this your mantra: *Cost Is An Issue Only In The Absence Of Value.*

Everything you do and say in an interview must communicate

your potential value to an organization, or you can't expect to be hired. Your ability to convey value will separate you from all others competing for the same job.

Think about your experience. You probably spend tremendous amounts of time, energy, or money on things that matter to you. Why do you spend more on one pair of shoes instead of another even though they have a similar look and feel and, of course, do the same thing? Was the tutor your parents retained to give your SAT scores a boost worth the cost? How about that private lacrosse coach? Some of these things are expensive, but we write the checks if we perceive value. Without value it's simply a cost.

Revisit those seven skills Tony Wagner identified as the ones corporations value most:

- Critical thinking and problem solving.
- Collaboration across networks and leading by influence.
- Agility and adaptability.
- Initiative and entrepreneurialism.
- Effective written and oral communications.
- Accessing and analyzing information.
- Curiosity and imagination.

The more of these skills an interviewer perceives you can bring to the party, the more value you represent, giving you a very good chance of winning the job.

3. You Are Not Your Résumé

Many interviews will begin with a simple request: "So tell me about yourself." It sounds like an easy enough way to begin a conversation. Right?

Believe it or not, while seemingly an innocuous request, how you respond sets the tone for your interview and might determine the outcome. In my experience most people respond incorrectly.

The mistake many people make is to refer back to their résumés, which one should assume the interviewer has already reviewed. If you do that, you are simply delivering an unnecessary recitation of what is already known.

I suggest a different approach. When you are asked the question, answer it with something like this:

> I see that you've read my résumé, so I won't take any of your valuable time rehashing what you already know. Unless you have any specific questions, I'd like to talk about what motivates me, my interests, the experiences that helped make me who I am, and how I decided that a career in _____ is the right one for me.

Wanting to know about you is perfectly reasonable for someone who has to decide if you are the right person for the job and a good fit for the organization. Your résumé is nothing more than a list of your education and professional experiences. If you are a recent graduate, it will probably be pretty sparse.

Answering the question in the way I've suggested gives you the opportunity to discuss your goals, problems you've encountered and solved, how you react in a crisis, and what you've accomplished of your own initiative.

Remember, everything on your résumé is a list of product features. Your job is to turn those features into benefits.

4. Don't Be Interrogated

Imagine you've been arrested, put in handcuffs, and taken to a windowless interrogation room somewhere in the bowels of the police station. You know how it works: detectives shine a light in your eyes and grill you with one question after another. The scene has played out so often on TV cop shows and in the movies, it's easy to imagine how unpleasant an interrogation must be. None of us wants to go through that experience, yet all too often we treat interviews like interrogations.

Interviews that are simple question-and-answer sessions are as stressful for the interviewers as they are for the candidates.

Employers are looking for adaptable, curious individuals who deal with stress by meeting any challenge with the confidence that there is a solution.

They are looking for leaders who are also team players. Above all employers are looking for individuals who will contribute to the success of the organization.

Answering questions without engaging in conversation will not communicate that you possess the critical skills that successful organizations value today. You must express confidence and project value by asking insightful questions and giving answers that invite a constructive discussion. Asking about a company's vacation policy does not communicate that you are looking for and can deal with challenge. Asking about an organization's position in its industry and steps it is taking to gain market share in a competitive environment does.

Taking control gives you a choice. You can allow an interview to feel like an interrogation or use it as an opportunity to engage in a constructive dialogue. The only difference between you and the individual interviewing you is that he or she has a job, and you don't. You don't like to be interrogated, and he or she doesn't want to be bored. Give him or her positive reasons to give your application serious consideration. Make a connection.

Remember, people like to talk about themselves. They also like talking about their organizations and what they do. Use this to your advantage. Show interest in interviewers. Use open-ended questions to encourage them to talk about themselves, their career paths, and their companies. In most cases by communicating, "I'm interested in you," you will set the stage for a constructive dialogue.

Doing so will dramatically shift the tone and direction of a conversation or interview. It's how friendships are created, and people do business with friends.

The biggest challenge you face in an interview is to set yourself apart from the crowd.

Sell your many assets.

Make yourself standout from the crowd.

Don't be a commodity.

The Bottom Line

- An interview is the ultimate sales pitch.
- The interview is never about you.
- You are not your resume.
- Don't be interrogated.
- The essence of an interview is the ability to convince a potential employer that you represent value to the organization.
- Cost is an issue in the absence of value.
- To win an interview your value has to resonate.
- Separate yourself from your competition.
- Employers aren't impulse buyers. In today's market they can afford to be selective.
- Luck has nothing to do with a job offer.
- Accent your assets (features) and how they benefit a prospective employer.
- Anticipate questions and/or objections, in advance.
- Prepare open-end questions in advance.
- Sell your unique qualifications.
- Never allow yourself to be a commodity.

CHAPTER 17
The Last Word

The American dream is under assault; we are our own worst enemy. You, the next generation of American leaders, must prepare for the challenge of keeping our nation strong.

It's time to embrace the kind of systematic change that is needed to ensure the American dream remains a reality.

Status quo is the enemy of progress.

The fact that so many recent graduates have difficulties finding jobs or have jobs that are well below their capabilities and training is clear evidence that we need to change the way we prepare students for the future. Systemic change is not easy, but Americans are used to tackling difficult challenges.

Most of us resist change. Handled poorly and without purpose, it causes consternation, disruption, and outright hostility. But change does not have to be painful. Change in pursuit of clearly defined goals, however, is visionary. Goals drive change. One thing is for certain: without clearly stated goals, there is no endgame. Goals represent destinations.

The best way to manage change is to break it into a series of steps that are necessary in order to reach a goal that everyone agrees is worthwhile. This requires buy-in, which means involving everyone in the planning process. Buy-in is achieved if those involved perceive individual and collective value in achieving the goal.

Goals matter. Properly decided upon and communicated, goals can be remarkably unifying—even transformative. Having a goal is having a purpose: change is simply an adjustment that is needed in order to achieve a goal. Goals mean we have our eyes on a prize.

If your parents truly want you to lead happy, productive lives doing what reflects your skills and interests, it's time to put their money where their mouths are. I think we can all agree that what we want for our kids was brilliantly summed up by former student, Nick Williams, who is now a wide receiver for the Atlanta Falcons: "I always imagine the feeling of achieving a lifelong dream. That feeling alone is worth fighting for every damn day."

Engage your parents as allies in a mission. Alliances form for mutually beneficial purposes, but purpose alone is not enough to make an alliance successful. In a sense alliances are self-serving; it takes time, negotiation, and unity of purpose to create visions and develop missions that truly unify the effort. Your parents need to curb their desire to drive the process. By being copilots on the journey, providing support and guidance when necessary, your parents empower you. You empower yourself when you set goals and create your own plan to achieve them.

Deep down inside each of us is the desire to be something, to make a positive difference.

Yet too many of us go through the motions. In a sense, they are running in place. Woody Allen has been credited with saying that eighty percent of life is just showing up. The tragedy is that by just showing up, you abdicate control of your life to other people or events instead of taking charge. This is not what you want. Individuals with a purpose are the ones making positive differences.

Think of the people you know who are happiest in their careers—those who truly embrace life, do interesting things, and have the most rewarding experiences. Those individuals are in control because they refuse to drift through life taking it as it comes. They never settle for just showing up.

As Steve Jobs advised Stanford graduates in his 2005 commencement address,

> Don't be trapped by dogma, which is living with the results of other people's thinking. Don't let the noise of others' opinions drown out your own inner voice. And most important, have the courage to follow your heart and intuition. They somehow already know what you truly want to become. Everything else is secondary.

Just wanting to want to emulate Steve Jobs does not make it happen. Jobs had a vision. He had goals. It might be said he wore them on his sleeve for all to see. In Jobs' view the ultimate goal is living a life of one's own creation, which means finding and living a passion, bypassing the life others would create for you.

Success rarely just happens. It takes planning and determination.

The more ambitious the goal, the more planning it will require. A goal provides a target; you have to reach for something to achieve anything. Too many people take life as it comes—the ones to whom Woody Allen referred. We all have dreams and ambitions. But most dreams come true only because our vision becomes a concrete plan of action. As nineteenth-century British Prime Minister Benjamin Disraeli said, "The secret of success in a man's life is to be ready for his opportunity when it comes."

What you want is for your parents to set the stage for you early. You exhibit interests and passions from an incredibly young age. Some childhood passions will wane; others might not. Instead of ignoring or dismissing these interests, you want your parents to nurture and encourage all of them. So what if as a ten-year-old you announce that you want to be a fireman instead of the attorney your parents hope you'll become? First, you're ten, and will probably change your mind. Second, it's your life. If your passion is to be a fireman that's exactly what you should do. You never want to look back and wonder "what if"?

Elevators up and down Wall Street belch out high-paid workers every day, their eyes fixed in thousand-yard stares. The looks on their faces embody what Thoreau meant when he said, "The mass of men lead lives of quiet desperation." They can't wait for the weekend and the opportunity to do what they really enjoy.

Someday many of your parents will look back at their careers and wonder, "what if." The process of deciding what you want to do in the future is serious business. Your parents can help by encouraging you to pursue your passions and helping you learn the fundamental yet essential skills that will pave the way to futures that embrace those passions. I call it creating an environment for success.

So why is this important? If we don't do it, your generation will be the first in American history to have a standard of living lower than that of your parents. The twentieth century is referred to as the American Century for good reason. In times of great challenge, when our very existence was threatened, Americans demonstrated uncanny abilities to adapt, meet any challenge, and prevail over those who would see us falter. Enlightened leadership, revolutionary thinking, and the ability to depart from dated concepts and theories are traits that made America great. Come to think of it, all we're really doing is getting back to basics.

Whether your dream is to make it to the NFL or to land an entry-level position at Facebook, successfully achieving the dream requires time and a collaborative effort. Students who are raised in collaborative, success-driven cultures start college at an advantage.

Jack Kerouac once observed, "Walking on water wasn't built in a day." Waiting until you are in college to learn the important life skills you will need to succeed in the post-college job scramble is too late. Your parent's goal should be to help you meet the increasingly competitive job market head on. You want to be prepared and empowered, and have confidence that you are ready for the future.

In a 2009 TED Talk, Simon Sinek, author of *Start with Why: How Great Leaders Inspire Everyone to Take Action*, observed that if "you hire people just because they can do a job, they'll work for money. But if you hire people who believe what you believe, they'll work for you with blood, sweat and tears."

The home environment in which you are raised should create the conditions under which you can find your interests and talents and receive the support and encouragement you need in order to flourish.

As the Chinese philosopher Lao-Tse observed, a journey of a thousand miles begins with a single step.

So what are you waiting for?

Acknowledgements

I learned a great deal in the process of writing *Taming Your Tiger Mom*. First and foremost, I now understand what it means to build a book -- word-by-word, chapter-by-chapter. Second, projects like this are not undertaken in a vacuum. This project required a lot of help. I am indebted to the many supportive individuals who proofread, offered constructive advice and criticism, and gave much-needed encouragement.

Special thanks to my incredible wife Ellen. Her editing, suggestions, and boundless patience have been invaluable.

Thank you Jim Medalia. It was Jim who first suggested that I use my career-coaching business as a springboard for a book. It was something I'd considered; Jim's urging got me to do it. Lifelong successful entrepreneurs, Jim and his wife E-Ping recently created a company called 225AM. com. The company, a career management toolkit for college students and graduates, provides much needed networking, organization, and step-by-step guidance.

Stephen King, CFO at WW Norton, provided valuable advice at a point when I was floundering. Beth Fitzgerald, founder of Fitzgerald Life Coaching, read the manuscript and offered many constructive suggestions. So did Kelly Gordon, Nancy Murphy, and Julia Anthony. My friend

Mike Morris, himself an author and editor provided invaluable guidance. I met Connie Glaser, the international best selling author of several books, including *GenderTalk Works*, at the exact point that I needed her advice and enthusiastic encouragement.

Many individuals read the manuscript at various stages of development. Thanks to: Stan Ward, Steve Corrsin, Rick and Mary Kelly, Emily DiCicco, Chris King, Barb Lauback, Gayle Pereira, Alli Cherry, Jared Atherton, Brendan Hurley, Lexi Golestani, Jordan Fusco, Gianna Crivelli, Joey Crivelli, Chris Yenney, Peter Stoddard, Holly Hargreaves, Ryan Furey, Mo Howard, Tate Libera Swanson, Carly Briggs, and my brothers Toby and Stephen Pitts for their suggestions. Thanks also to my friend Mike Sciortino. Mike, a former colleague, is the author of the recently published best seller, *Gratitude Marketing*.

Scores of individuals shared personal experiences and anecdotes. Thanks to Eric Melniczek, Joan Roux, Etienne Roux, Jeremi Roux, Bryan Matthews, Ryan Kreger, Isabelle Kristiansen, Nick Nicolls, Angela Rieder, Allayna Garret, Tyler Willey, A. R. Willey, Ruth Williams, Nick Williams, Mike Williams, Liz Colicchio, Jeff Batt, Elaine Gampel, and Jim Bruton. Unfortunately, not every story was used, but each in its own way helped me build this book. If I've forgotten anyone I sincerely apologize.

Finally, I want to thank the good folks at Small World Coffee in Princeton, New Jersey, Café Espresso in Savannah, Georgia, and Cutter's Point Coffee in Sandfly, Georgia. Not only do each serve great coffee, they were generous enough to let me spend countless hours, monopolizing a table, as I tried to figure out how to write a book.

Tim Pitts earned his BA from Roanoke College and an MA from New York University.

Pitts spent twenty-five years in financial services, as an investment executive and sales manager. For the last ten years of his career he was chairman of OppenheimerFunds Distributors.

After leaving the investment business, Pitts pursued his passions for travel, history, and photography for several years before joining the faculty at The Hun School of Princeton. He taught Cold War history, global problems, and leadership.

In 2008 he founded Shameless Self Promotion to help recent college graduates with their careers.

Pitts and his wife, Ellen, live in Savannah, Georgia, where he volunteers as a medical first responder.

CPSIA information can be obtained at www.ICGtesting.com
Printed in the USA
LVOW10s1206240116

472053LV00020B/537/P